HOW TO BE A
LANDLORD

Team Incredible Publishing

HOW TO BE A LANDLORD

The definitive guide to letting and managing your rental property

Rob Dix

CONTENTS

INTRODUCTION

After spending years working in property, I've noticed that there are two distinct tribes of property owners.

First, there are the "landlords". They want to make money from their property, of course, but they also enjoy showing it off at viewings, interacting with tenants and dealing with all the odd jobs that come up.

Then there are the "investors". These are the people who view their property as a money-making machine, are led by the numbers, and don't really want to have anything to do with its day-to-day running. They take pride in offering a good service, but they want *someone else* to provide that service and don't really give a monkey's about getting a Christmas card from their tenants.

It's not the case that one tribe is right and the other is wrong. But I do think that *both* often put themselves at risk by not knowing enough about the details of managing a property.

Because those details are important. After all, you're taking one of the most expensive assets you'll ever own and handing it over to a stranger to live in – and in the process, giving them a whole series of rights that are governed by hundreds of different laws. You might be surprised to learn that forgetting to provide a certain piece of paper can prevent you from removing non-paying tenants, or that you can be imprisoned for not checking a tenant's passport, or that it could be considered harassment if you ring the doorbell without giving 24 hours' notice... but it's true. Strangely, all the people lining up to tell you "how to make a fortune in property" disappear pretty sharpish when it gets to the boring but important things you need to know to avoid some pretty unpleasant fates.

You're not absolved from caring about all of this if you hand everything over to a letting agent, either – because as the property owner, the ultimate legal liability remains with you. And given the variable quality of letting agents, you could end up paying a fee that goes beyond "reassuringly expensive" and *still* find that your agent is breaking laws you didn't even know existed.

ABOUT THIS BOOK

This book is my attempt to fill in those important details, for both hands-on landlords and those who would rather put someone else in charge – in a way that's straightforward, non-intimidating and (in places) even entertaining.

This book doesn't cover how to find the right property to rent out in the first place: it assumes you have a property that you've bought, are in the process of buying, or that you currently live in and intend to rent out.

Buying the right property in the first place is an enormous topic, and I've written a whole other book about it – The Complete Guide To Property Investment (www.propertygeek.net/completeguide). If you don't want to read a whole other book, I've put together a free video course about "Running The Numbers" on a potential property investment, and it's available at www.thepropertyhub.net/courses

Once you own the property, this book will walk you through every step: preparing it to let, advertising for tenants, conducting viewings, doing all the paperwork, managing the tenancy and dealing with any tricky situations that crop up. You might want to read it through once to get the overall picture, then dip back into individual sections as you go through and do it for real.

Many of the tasks involved in letting a property are purely procedural – but there are also plenty where there's no "right" answer, and every landlord will have their own way of doing it. So rather than just pushing *my* way, I've drawn on the experience of 64 different self-managing landlords while putting this book together. You'll find them all listed at the end, and I've pulled out specific words of wisdom as "Pro tips" throughout the text.

No individual part of the process is that hard – there's just a lot of it. If you decide after reading that it's actually a bit *too* much, I've included a bonus chapter about how to pick the right letting agent – and after reading about everything they'll be doing for you, you might have a newfound appreciation for how hard they (should) work to earn their money.

Note: Unless specifically stated otherwise, everything in this book refers to renting a property in England or Wales to an individual, couple or single family. At the end, you'll find bonus chapters covering letting properties in Scotland, and the legalities around properties that are let to multiple unrelated occupants – known as Houses in Multiple Occupation, or HMOs.

ABOUT ME

I've owned buy-to-let property for about ten years. I started out as a pretty hands-on landlord, and I enjoyed the challenge of learning how everything worked and solving problems when they came up. And, to be honest, I was probably too much of a control freak to hand over control to anyone else.

As I've become busier with other ventures and my portfolio has grown, I've become a pure "investor". All my properties are managed, and some of them I've never even been inside.

But property management is actually a bigger part of my life now than ever before, because I now co-own Yellow Lettings (www.yellowlettings.net) – an agency that lets and manages hundreds of properties across England.

Starting the agency forced me to improve my knowledge, as I took a qualification that allowed our agency to become a member of the ARLA regulation scheme. But more importantly, it's given me an unusual level of exposure to everything that managing a property involves – from the highs of getting thank you cards from tenants, to the lows of enormous leaks in the ceiling late at night, to the thoroughly bizarre situations that crop up far more often than you might expect.

As well as Yellow Lettings, I co-founded the free property community The Property Hub (www.thepropertyhub.net), co-present the UK's most popular business podcast – The Property Podcast (www.thepropertyhub.net/podcast) – and own a bridging finance company called LendSwift (www.lendswift.co.uk). You can find out more about everything I do at www.propertygeek.net

STAY UPDATED

Given how often legislation changes, writing a book about letting and management is pretty much the worst idea ever for an author who wants to just sit back and watch the royalties roll in. Honestly, I think my next book will be about a young billionaire wizard who's into S&M or something.

But because I'm a sucker for punishment (and more than a little bit geeky), I'm committing to keeping this book up-to-date. **All you need to do is register your copy of this book, and I'll send you an email whenever there's a change I think you should know about.**

You'll receive lots of other goodies too:

- A list of all the providers I recommend for services like insurance, referencing and furniture. (I don't include these recommendations in the book itself because they could change over time – so by giving you a separate list, I can keep it updated and you'll always have access to the latest version.)

- A printable checklist of all the major tasks you need to

perform when renting out a property, so you won't accidentally miss any important steps.

- An email when I give the book its annual update, with the full text of all the sections that have changed as well as a summary of the smaller tweaks.

It'll cost you exactly nothing – all you need to do is register your copy at www.propertygeek.net/landlord

PART 1:
PREPARING YOUR PROPERTY TO LET

Introduction

So! You have a property that you want to rent out.

Maybe you bought it, maybe you inherited it, or perhaps you're moving out of your own home and looking to rent it out. Whatever the situation, you're probably eager to find some tenants and get the rent rolling in.

Not so fast! There's some groundwork to be done before we get to all that.

I've never known a global bestseller to start with a whole section on safety, insurance and permissions, but I'm scuppering my Booker Prize chances on your behalf: it's critical that you get all this stuff in order to avoid problems down the line. So let's get to it…

Chapter 1

Consents and permissions

Before committing to the hard work of getting the property ready to let, let's start by making sure that you're actually *allowed* to rent the property out. While you might take the view that it's your property and you can do what you bloomin' well like with it, that's not necessarily the case. So unless you relish living on the edge, you should make sure you've obtained permission from other relevant parties.

> *Pro tip: "Get to know the neighbours soon after you buy. Owner-occupiers are understandably wary about there being a buy-to-let next door, but if you introduce yourself and make nice, you'll have an ally who can give you a heads-up if external maintenance issues aren't brought to your attention early." –Muna Nwokolo*

Consent from the freeholder

If you're the leaseholder rather than the freeholder of the property, you'll need to get permission from whoever owns the freehold (or whoever is managing it on the freeholder's behalf). In the vast majority of cases, you'll be a leaseholder if you own a flat and a freeholder if you buy a house.

As a leaseholder, you'll have a lease agreement (which you'll have received when you bought the property) that sets out what you can and can't do with it. It's unusual for leases to say that you're not allowed to let the property out at all, but they might have stipulations about the type of tenancy you can issue. So check your lease – and if you've owned the property for a while and can't find it, contact your freeholder or their management company (this will be whoever sends you those unpleasant letters demanding a service charge and/or ground rent from you).

The leaseholder will often ask for a fee to "register" the sublet (basically just writing you a very expensive letter saying "OK, go for it!"), the amount of which is sometimes stated in the lease and sometimes not. If your lease doesn't state the fee payable to register a sublet and they start demanding crazy amounts of money from you, it's worth pushing back and seeing if they reconsider. (Remember: they're entitled to know how you intend to use the property because they technically still own it and have just leased it to you. But charging more than £50 to register the fact that you've told them is just daft in my book. Which this is.)

Registration and licenses

Increasingly, owning a rental property means either registering yourself with the local authority or obtaining a license from them, or both.

Registration is about assessing whether you're a suitable individual to be letting a property. It tends to just be a form-filling exercise, only needs to be done once for each local authority, and doesn't expire.

A license will also look at whether you're suitable as a person, but it'll also impose conditions upon how the property is run and maintained. Licenses tend to be granted for up to five years, and the property could be inspected to check that the conditions are being met.

When it comes to legislation, the direction of travel tends to be one-way – so I wouldn't be at all surprised if licensing became mandatory everywhere in the UK within the next five years. For now, though, it differs depending on where the property is located – so let's run through the different situations.

Properties in Wales

If you let out a property anywhere in Wales, you need to register with a scheme called Rent Smart Wales. This can be done online at www.rentsmart.gov.wales, and just involves supplying a few personal details and paying a fee.

(We're only a few pages into this book and this is already our second mention of unexpected fees. Get used to it: the longer you spend in the landlording game the more you'll come to expect to be charged surprising amounts of money for odd bits of paper.)

If you plan to *self-manage* the property (which means either finding tenants or managing the tenancy yourself, rather than using a letting agent for both), you *also* need to obtain a license. This involves paying *another* fee, declaring yourself to be a fit and proper person, and completing some training – which can be done online or in person.

The scheme is still in its infancy, and details and prices are likely to keep changing – so rather than getting into the nitty gritty here, it's best if you just go to www.rentsmart.gov.wales to get the full details.

Properties in Scotland

For properties let in Scotland, you need to register with the local authority via www.landlordregistrationscotland.gov.uk

You'll (you guessed it) have to pay a fee, provide some basic information and be judged to be a fit and proper person.

Unlike in Wales, you *don't* need to obtain a separate license and undergo training if you're going to be self-managing. Whether you're going it alone or using an agent, registration is all you need.

Selective licensing in England

In England there's no nationwide registration or licensing requirement, but there is a trend towards "selective licensing" –

meaning that individual councils can decide to insist on a license being granted for either the entire local authority area or specific areas where anti-social behaviour has been a problem.

You can find out if this applies to the area where your property is located by Googling "[council name] landlord licensing" and seeing if anything comes up. Alternatively, you can give your local housing department a call.

Obtaining a license is another annoying cost and admin exercise, but it generally isn't difficult if you need one. You just have to fill in a form, pay a fee, and agree to maintain certain standards – which might be confirmed by an inspection. Each area is allowed to choose how much to charge, but it's fairly typical for licenses to be issued for five years and cost in the range of £250 to £600. In Croydon – the most expensive I'm aware of – it's £850.

The supposed point of selective licensing, in case you were wondering, is to raise standards in rental accommodation and reduce antisocial behaviour. This seems bizarre to pretty much everyone because the conditions of the license are very similar to the legal duties that landlords have under housing law anyway, and what any of it has to do with antisocial behaviour is a complete mystery. It's also pointless because local authorities don't have anywhere near the resources to inspect every rental property or even track down the ones that are unlicensed, but still: if you need a license, go and get one.

Council tax

While we're talking about local authorities… it's worth quickly noting that if you've just bought the property, you'll be liable for the council tax from the day of completion until the day it's let out – and when the tenants move out, you'll be liable for any gap before new tenants move in. Seriously: given what local authorities are usually like, they're astonishingly efficient when it comes to getting a council tax demand through the door the second a property becomes empty.

Some councils offer short-term exemptions for properties that are empty or undergoing refurbishment – but, of course, you'll need to make the council aware of the situation or they'll automatically bill you for the full amount. Check the local authority's website to find out what the rules are, and there will often be an online form you can submit to claim an exemption. (In my experience, they're less startlingly efficient when it comes to processing exemptions, so it's worth checking the bill that comes through and calling to query it if you think it's wrong.)

Registering with HMRC

While you're going through all this effort with the aim of making some rental income, you won't get to keep all of it: you'll need to give a healthy slice of it to the government.

If the property you're renting out is owned within a limited company, there's nothing you need to do at this point: your company will just start filing its accounts, tax returns and annual confirmation statements as they become due.

There's also no action needed if you own the property as an individual but you already submit a self-assessment tax return – for example, because you're self-employed. In this case you'll just report your property income on the tax return you'd be submitting anyway.

But if you're currently taxed solely via PAYE (and you don't, therefore, submit a self-assessment return), you'll need to inform HMRC that you're going to have income from property to declare. There are various contact methods, which you can find on the gov.uk website.

If your income from property is less than £2,500 after allowable expenses, you won't need to fill in a self-assessment tax return but you *do* still need to notify them. For higher amounts, you will need to start submitting an annual tax return – which you can either do yourself or hire an accountant to do for you.

If you live overseas...

There are more fun and games if you're classed as an "overseas landlord", which is defined as someone who spends more than six months of each year outside the UK.

If you're an overseas landlord and you don't fill in the form I mention in a moment, your tenant (or letting agent, if you use one) should deduct the basic rate of tax before passing your rental income to you. This isn't ideal, because your tax still won't be correct: you'll be overpaying because you'll have expenses that won't have been accounted for, and also under-paying if you should have been taxed at a higher rate.

(Also, it seems thoroughly bizarre that a tenant should be forced to become an unpaid tax collector just because they're living in a property that happens to be owned by someone who spends time abroad.)

I can only assume all this nonsense made sense to someone, at some point – but if you want to (wisely) avoid it, you can submit an application to receive your income gross and sort out the tax by self-assessment later. You'll need to fill in the NRL1i form (which you can find by searching the gov.uk website), and in most circumstances they'll write to approve your application and give you further guidance.

If the property is owned by an overseas *company* (meaning one incorporated outside the UK and with no place of business in the UK), the process is the same but you need to use form NRL2i instead.

In theory at least, if you don't use a letting agent, your tenant is still expected to register with HMRC and file an annual report even if you've successfully applied to be paid the rent without tax deducted. Presumably some tenant somewhere is diligently doing this, but I rarely come across a landlord who's even aware of this requirement – let alone one who coaches their tenant through doing it.

Consent from your mortgage lender

If you have a mortgage on the property, it's crucial that your lender knows you'll be letting the property out and is happy for you to do so.

In certain property investment circles, there's a belief that the lender "doesn't care as long as they're getting paid every month", but this isn't even close to being true. Sure, they might not notice for years, or even forever – but that doesn't mean they don't care. And if they *do* notice, the worst case is pretty bad: they could demand that you immediately repay the loan in full, and take action to repossess the property if you don't. Not cool.

Let's take a quick look at the two main scenarios you'll be in when it comes to getting the go-ahead from your lender to let a property. Remember, though, that this is only a quick overview: the world of mortgages is extremely complex and the stakes are high, so if you're in any doubt you should take advice from a good mortgage adviser.

If you've bought the property specifically to rent out...

In this situation, you should have bought the property using a specialist buy-to-let mortgage, so the lender is clearly happy for the property to be rented out.

However, that still doesn't mean you can do whatever you like: the lender will have made certain stipulations in your mortgage offer about the types of tenant they're happy for you to rent the property out to. Some restrictions that you'll often see are:

- You can only rent the property on an Assured Shorthold Tenancy (AST) with a fixed duration of less than a year (don't worry – we'll get into exactly what this means in Part 3).

- You can't rent the property to tenants who are in receipt of Housing Benefit.

- You can't rent rooms out individually – the whole property must be covered by a single AST.

- You can only rent the property to a single family – not to friends (or strangers) sharing, even if they're all on the same AST.

These sorts of restrictions will be stated in your mortgage offer, so refer back to that if you're not sure what your lender is happy for you to do.

If you've used a good mortgage adviser and given them all the relevant information, they should have ensured that your mortgage product is suitable for your plans. It's worth keeping in mind, though, that if you ever decide to change the type of tenant (for example, you might want to rent out rooms individually, having previously rented to a single family), you'll need to ask your lender's permission – and you might need to switch to a different lender if they refuse.

If you're renting the property you currently live in

This scenario covers you if you're an "accidental" landlord – for example, you need to move to a different area for work but haven't been able to sell your house, or you've decided to move to a larger property but want to keep your old home to rent out.

If you've previously been living in the property, you'll have a residential mortgage, which means that the lender expects you to be living there as your main home and has not agreed for you to rent it out.

At this point, you might assume that – as long as you keep paying the mortgage – the lender won't notice if you just rent the property out. *This is not the case:* lenders run checks against the electoral roll to see if anyone is registered as living at the property who shouldn't be, and they've even been known to knock on the door to check!

So don't do that. (And also, don't do the converse and live in a property that you have a buy-to-let mortgage on. If anything, that's even worse.)

Instead, do this:

Obtain consent to let

Lenders are often happy to give you permission to rent the property out for a limited period of time, because they're aware that circumstances change and they don't want to punish "accidental" landlords. If you speak to your lender, they'll often agree to give you consent to let for anything up to a few years.

Sometimes they'll increase your interest rate slightly, or some-times they'll allow you to stay on the same rate for a certain period of time (like six months or a year) before they increase the rate. If you're lucky, there might be no increase in rate at all, but there will often be a small administration fee to issue consent.

Switch to a buy-to-let mortgage

This will be your only option if you're either:

- Buying a new property to live in while keeping your old one (because you won't be able to have two residential mortgages at the same time)

Or:

- Unable to get consent to let

This isn't the place to get into the ins and outs of buy-to-let mortgages – and I'd recommend speaking to a good broker – but there are a few things to keep in mind:

- You can typically (at the time of writing) only get buy-to-let mortgages to cover up to 75% of the property's value – so if you have a residential mortgage with a balance outstanding that's more than 75% of the property's value, you might struggle to switch.

- Unlike with residential mortgages, the most important factor in lending is the income the property produces rather than the income *you* earn. Lenders will typically want the rent to be at least 125% (sometimes up to 145%) of what the monthly mortgage payment would be if the interest rate were at least 5.5%, although criteria differ.

  For example, if you borrowed £100,000 on an interest-only basis, the annual mortgage payment at an interest rate of 5.5% would be £5,500 – so if the lender required coverage of 145%, the annual rent would need to be at least £7,975. This could cause you an issue if you have an expensive property that generates relatively little rent.

- The good news is that you can get a buy-to-let mortgage on an "interest only" basis (whereas your residential mortgage is probably on a "capital repayment" basis), which will reduce your monthly payments.

Again, if you *do* find yourself needing to switch to a buy-to-let mortgage, I'd strongly advise getting help from a broker – preferably one who specialises in buy-to-let rather than residential mortgages (they really are totally different ball games). The broker should also have access to the whole of the market rather than be tied to offering products from just a subset of lenders. Their fee will be somewhere in the region of £300 to £600, which is nothing compared to the money you can save by choosing the right product.

Chapter 2

Making the property shipshape

Whether you've just bought a property or are renting out somewhere that's previously been your home, there may well be some degree of work needed to bring it up to scratch before it can be let out. I don't pretend to be an expert on any labour heavier than tapping away on a keyboard, but in this section I'll cover some of the very basic points to consider when a refurb is needed.

If you do have a refurb coming up, you might want to consider becoming a member of LNPG – a "buying club" for landlords that allows individuals to get trade prices (and sometimes even lower) from major suppliers of kitchens, bathrooms, plumbing supplies and all sorts of other materials. I've had big savings on bathrooms and boilers in the past – and if you don't save enough to cover the annual fee, they'll roll your membership over to the next year. They've given me a code that gets you a discount of 10% on your membership, which I'll send you when you register your book at www.propertygeek.net/landlord

Pro tip: "My wife and I spent a night in one property before we let it out. A lot of little things – like the need for hooks on the backs of doors – aren't obvious until you spend a night in a property yourself. We also found that using the shower in the morning tripped the electrics – which only happened after a few minutes of use, so we wouldn't have known otherwise." –Gareth Broom

Finding a builder and getting quotes

A network of trusted contractors is one of a landlord's most valuable assets… but it's not something you're likely to have when starting out. If you've got a friend, family member or random Facebook acquaintance in the trades, I thoroughly recommend buying them a few boxes of Milk Tray and thanking them for their very thoughtful career choice. If not, now's the time to start auditioning people to take care of all those pre-tenancy jobs.

Personal recommendations will always be the best way to find the right person, so consider attending a few local property networking events: other landlords might be willing to share the highlights of their little black book with you.

Failing that, there's no need to resort to the Yellow Pages (if that even still exists). I like using websites where you can post your job and have interested tradespeople reply: MyBuilder.com, Checkatrade.com and RatedPeople.com are a few of the biggest. In addition to the massive upside that you don't have to make multiple phone calls (because tradespeople come to you instead), another big benefit is that tradespeople are rated on the site by their past clients.

On balance, I'd still take a personal recommendation – but being able to see that somebody has reviews from 50 happy customers certainly gives me a good amount of confidence. Some reviews can be faked, but even the most enthusiastic self-promoter only has so many aunties and uncles to pad out their ratings.

However you find a potential tradesperson, make sure you do the following:

- Check that they hold appropriate professional indemnity insurance (they should be willing to show you their certificate without any grumbles or excuses).

- See if they belong to the appropriate trade body (which gives some confidence in their standards, and also – as we'll see in the next section – makes life easier with the local authority).

- Search for the company name and the name of the individual you've spoken to, to make sure nobody's complained about them or reviewed them poorly elsewhere. Do go beyond the first couple of pages of results, just in case they're a shoddy builder but great at online marketing.

- Speak to a couple of their previous clients, if the job is big enough to justify the time doing so.

Unless the job is tiny, it's always a good idea to get three quotes

– and you should make sure you're clear on the exact scope of work that each job covers. If they're also supplying the materials, you should also get them to clarify exactly what materials are being supplied. For example, if one quote for a new bathroom is twice the price of another, is that because they're supplying a much more expensive suite – or do they just have a higher day rate? For anything where personal taste is a factor, dictating what materials should be used (whether you or they are sourcing them) is probably a good idea.

Don't be afraid to ask for more clarity and specificity in the quote – so rather than just saying "replace bathroom", it says what is being installed, what units there will be, what the floor covering will be, if any radiators will be replaced, and so on. It's the only way you'll be able to know that you're going to get what you want, and be able to hold them to it if they don't deliver.

You should also make sure you know when they'll be able to start the work and how long they think it should take, and get this in writing. It's no good finding a cheap quote then having to wait a month until they can start – meaning that by the time you've accounted for a month of lost rental income, it ends up being very expensive.

For big jobs, you ought to have a proper contract with clear specifications, dates, figures and provisions for when things go wrong. The Federation of Master Builders has put together a template, which I'll send you when you register your copy of this book at www.propertygeek.net/landlord

Building regulations and planning approval

When doing any kind of work, it's important to know whether your plans will require approval in terms of building regulations, planning permission, or both.

Let's take building regulations first. They exist to make sure you adhere to safety standards when you want to:

- Put up a new building

- Extend or alter an existing one

- In the words of the government's planning portal, "Provide services and/or fittings in a building such as washing and sanitary facilities, hot water cylinders, foul water and rainwater drainage, replacement windows, and fuel burning appliances of any type"

The planning portal I just quoted from has a useful list of common projects that require building regulations approval: www.-planningportal.gov.uk/permission/commonprojects

If you're using a tradesperson, it's their responsibility to get approval from the building regulations department of the local authority, and they'll also be the ones to face a fine if they don't. This still wouldn't be good for you, however, because as the owner of the building you could be ordered to undo or remedy unapproved works at your own expense.

If the tradesperson is a "competent person" (meaning that they're a member of a trade body scheme, like FENSA for windows or ECA for electrics), they can self-certify that their work meets buildings standards without having to invite in the local authority to inspect the job afterwards. They'll issue you with a certificate stating that the work is compliant, which becomes very important when you come to sell or refinance the property: I've had a mortgage application held up in the past because I'd installed new windows and the fitter had forgotten to give me the certificate.

Doing the work yourself? Then it's your responsibility to get approval before doing the works and have them signed off afterwards, so check the planning portal to see what you need to do.

Then there's planning permission. In addition to building regulations approval, you might also need permission from the local authority for projects that involve a new construction, extension, or a change of use.

Some projects will fall under "permitted development", meaning you don't need to seek permission. Again, the government portal's list of common projects (www.planningportal.gov.uk/permission/commonprojects) will tell you if the project meets the criteria for permitted development or whether you need to apply for planning permission.

Even if the project appears not to require planning permission, it's still a good idea to contact the local authority to check before going ahead: you might be restricted for various other reasons. For example, the property might be in a conservation area, or the local authority might have issued something called an Article 4 Direction – which means they've locally withdrawn certain permitted development rights that apply nationally.

Deciding on the spec

When it comes to deciding on exactly what a refurb should involve, there are two big mistakes that people tend to make again and again.

The first is installing fixtures and fittings that are far more expensive than they need to be. A "rental refurb" is very different from what you'd have in your own home, or a property you were hoping to sell for top dollar.

As a general rule, go for "sturdy" over "fancy". Most people over-spec their first property by having the best of intentions about creating a great place to live – only to break out in a cold sweat when they discover a chip in their extremely expensive bath. You'll also find that nobody is going to pay a penny more in rent just because the carpet has fibres that were lovingly hand-twisted by Norwegian artisans – so don't scrimp, but don't over-spend on things that don't matter.

The key is to let the market dictate what the standard of the finish should be. You can get a sense of what your market requires by looking at similar "let agreed" properties on Right-move and seeing what they have in common, or asking other local landlords.

The other big mistake is imposing your personal taste on the property. Yes, your taste is utterly brilliant, of course, but this isn't about *your* taste: it's about providing the sort of decor that's been shown again and again to work in rental properties. That means clean, bright and functional – like white walls (perhaps with a feature wall), light brown carpets, and any furnishings you're providing being as neutral as possible too.

To be clear: your own house may well have been awarded "House Of The Year" on Grand Designs, and it may epitomise quality and class, but replicating it in your rental property won't do you any favours.

Beyond the general principles of not over-doing the spec and not imposing your own taste, what else should you be consider-ing when deciding how to kit out a property for the rental market?

It's hard to say, because whenever landlords get together there are often surprisingly fractious debates about fixtures and fittings – and no one ever seems able to agree on the "best way" to do anything. This is often due to people forming opinions based on isolated bad experiences, but it's also because it's so dependent on your tenant demographic: what looks superb in one property might be not hard-wearing enough for another.

Nevertheless, after gathering opinions from over 50 different landlords, I've put together a list of recommendations that seem to have broad consensus…

Bathrooms

Shower trays are notoriously leaky, so a shower over a bath can lead to fewer problems. Even if there's a separate shower cubicle, having a shower attachment over the bath makes for a useful backup.

You might also want to consider an electric shower if you've got the choice: it means that even if the boiler isn't working, your tenants can still have hot showers.

Where possible, it could be worth putting in more than one bathroom – or an extra separate toilet if space is tight. It means that if one toilet breaks, there's still another to use – so the repair isn't an emergency as it would otherwise be.

> *Pro tip: "When you first buy a property, change anything that looks old or 'on the way out' – like power showers, central heating pumps that thump and make lots of noise, and radiators that have obviously leaked at the seams. It's much easier to fix these in advance with one contractor visit than to wait for something to go wrong and have to fix it under pressure." –Richard Springall*

Kitchens

You've probably heard the old adage that kitchens and bathrooms sell properties. The same is true when it comes to renting, but that doesn't mean you need to go all-out on granite work surfaces.

If you're inheriting an old kitchen, you don't necessarily have to rip it out and start again: it's possible that just replacing the cupboard doors will be enough to give the whole room a lift. If you *are* putting in a new kitchen, avoid integrated appliances unless the spec needs to be extremely high-end for your target demographic: they look better, but they're more difficult and expensive to repair when they go wrong.

Flooring

Don't blow the budget on flooring, because the chances of it being looked after with appropriate care are somewhere between "five lottery numbers" and "England World Cup win".

Good-quality laminate can be hard-wearing in high-traffic areas like hallways, and can also be suitable for the living room – especially if tenants eat in there. It will still collect scratches and scrapes, but these can be artfully disguised with a child's crayon (seriously) or fixed with a repair kit. The main drawback is that most laminate soaks up water and warps if it gets wet, so if tenants use a mop on it (or even just have a major spill), life might start getting bumpy.

Carpets are a tricky one because dark carpets don't tend to look great, but light carpets show every mark. Most people go for beige or cappuccino, but a darker grey can work too. Cheap carpet can be made to feel a lot better underfoot with a thick underlay.

I'm all for tiling kitchen and bathroom floors: it looks best and is hard-wearing, and the odd broken tile can be replaced easily enough.

Laminate is a good choice too, but avoid anything too cheap: in bathrooms it will be affected by moisture, and in kitchens you'll need something thick so it doesn't rip when tenants drag out appliances to clean (or more likely, to retrieve their dropped iPhone) behind them.

> Pro tip: "I always seal my floors in kitchens, bathrooms and wet areas – so if using laminate flooring, I'll silicone a 10–15mm bead all around the perimeter. It means that if someone uses a mop, there wont be any edge leakage into sub-floors or ceilings below. You can guarantee the tenant and cleaning services will be heavy-handed – so protect against it from the off where possible." – Adrian Bond

Walls

I'm a fan of painting straight onto the walls if the plaster is good enough: lining paper is a faff, and it can start lifting away from the wall after a few coats. A good plastering job upfront can save a lot of hassle later on.

If there's already wallpaper that you can paint over, that can be fine as long as your target market doesn't require the decoration to be absolutely perfect. Textured wallpaper is a whole other conversation: I can't stand it, but if it's not going to affect the rentability of the property (or the amount you can charge), it doesn't seem worth the hassle and expense of replacing it. Plus if you hold onto the property long enough, it might even become fashionable again at some point.

In terms of colour, some variety of white or light grey will do the job – and if you use the same colour everywhere (and in every property, if you have more than one), touching up marks will be easy and you won't have to juggle multiple half-empty tins. Make sure you use the same brand each time too, as even colours with the same name can vary slightly between manufacturers.

You can also consider adding an accent wall – think grey rather than hot pink – in the living room, to dial down the sterile "beige box" vibe that rental properties sometimes have. Again, this can be the same in all properties to cut down on hassle when it comes to re-painting.

In kitchens and bathrooms, use water-resistant eggshell or acrylic paint: it will wipe clean if it gets splashed, and won't be affected by excess moisture.

Electrics

If you're going to be doing electrical work anyway, take the opportunity to make sure there are plenty of sockets and that they're in convenient places (at least one on each wall in every room): it's much safer than having your tenants move in and trail extension cables everywhere.

These days, almost every type of tenant will be juggling multiple mobile devices – so you could also consider adding USB plug sockets. It won't make or break anyone's decision about whether to rent the property, but it's a nice touch.

Safety

If you're going to be doing work to a new property anyway, it's worth installing hard-wired smoke detectors and carbon monoxide alarms while you're at it. You could also put a heat detector in the kitchen (where you wouldn't be able to fit a smoke detector, because steam from cooking would set it off).

As we'll see in the upcoming section on safety requirements, hard-wired detectors aren't mandatory and carbon monoxide alarms may not be either – but there's no reason not to make the property that bit safer anyway.

Also, fit handrails on any staircases that don't already have them. Not only is it safer, but insurers will often refuse to pay out on claims relating to falls if there isn't a handrail – so the small cost is worth it twice over.

Gardens

A nice garden can be a selling point for some types of tenant, but most aren't interested in keeping it tidy and it can quickly turn into a jungle.

You obviously can't remove a garden if there already is one, but you'll save yourself a lot of work if you pave as much of it as possible.

If there's no off-street parking and it's possible to convert part of the front garden for this purpose, it's worth considering too: most tenants will favour convenience over aesthetics.

Overseeing the project

Depending on the size of the project and your own particular skill set, you might decide to manage the project yourself and hire in individual trades, or hire one main contractor who'll serve as project manager and sub-contract any jobs that they can't take on themselves. You could also bring in a dedicated project manager (who isn't also the main contractor), who will normally charge around 10% of the total works cost as their fee.

If you choose to manage a big project yourself, you'll need to have detailed knowledge of the construction process, as well as stellar communication and organisational skills. Being the project manager is a tough job, and – unless you have previous building experience – the thought of doing it probably scares the life out of you. There's a school of thought that says you should manage your first major job yourself, because you'll learn so much that it will stand you in good stead for all future projects (even if you choose to hire someone else to project manage in future). I understand the logic, but clearly it's not something I subscribe to myself.

Even if you recognise your limitations (whether that's time or experience) and put someone else in charge, remember: you're still the boss. As with everything in life, the squeaky wheel gets the grease. The reality is that builders are usually juggling multiple jobs, and if you're not on top of them it's easy for your project to be the one that falls to the bottom of the pile. The jobs I've seen go the most wrong are the ones where the investor put someone in charge and expected to come back a couple of months later to a totally finished project. Instead, they tended to find that the builders had got as far as making everything a total mess, but stopped short of putting it back together again.

So, whatever the arrangement, make sure you're a constant presence. Be on the phone every day, and on site as often as you can. Don't get in the way or be prematurely aggressive, but do show through your actions that you're on top of things and will give them earache if things slip.

Overseeing the project also means keeping an eye on the time and the budget. Let's be real here: the likelihood is that your project *will* go over both. The solution is to make sure you've factored that in from the start.

In other words, if a job *absolutely must* be done in two months' time, agree with all involved that it needs to be done in a month. Even if everyone has the best of intentions and works as hard as possible, unexpected delays will always creep in. Whether it's weather, delays with materials or unexpected complications arising, I've yet to see a project of any size that runs exactly as you'd expect it to in an ideal world.

The same goes for the budget, because time and money are very closely linked when it comes to building projects. To minimise the chances of the budget running out of control, agree on a fixed-price quote at the start and state the milestones at which payments will be made. This will also help to keep the project running on time, as they'll always have the incentive to get the next bit done to release the payment. Whatever you do, *don't* get comfortable and start paying instalments ahead of what has actually been done and approved: standards can start to slip at any point, however diligent your builder seems to be.

Even with a fixed-price quote, legitimate unexpected expenses will crop up that go beyond the agreed scope of the job – and that's why you should always mentally budget for a contingency fund. The level of financial contingency you set is up to you, but I suggest 20%. It's on the pessimistic end of the scale, but that's the point: the absolute worst thing that can happen is to run out of money before you can finish, so you need to be able to cope with any reasonable eventuality.

> Pro tip: "Check and test everything before tenants move in. I've had a plasterer accidentally leave a bit of plaster in a new socket so you can't get the plug in; and a plumber who hasn't connected the pipework for the dishwasher properly, or has fitted the wrong low-pressure bath taps. Now I check everything as soon as any work is completed, and often find issues that you might not notice until a tenant moves in. I plug a lamp or similar into every socket, run

any new electrical appliances, run all taps, fill the bath, run the shower, and turn all radiators on full. I even keep an old TV and Freeview box and test all aerial sockets." –Gary Brewin

Chapter 3

Furnished or unfurnished?

Now that your property is in tip-top decorative order, should you steel yourself to drive to the edge of town and spend the afternoon getting hopelessly lost and frustrated at Ikea? (But if you do, hey: cheap meatballs!)

Really, the answer should be dictated by your target tenant market rather than your personal tolerance for shopping. If you're renting a three-bed semi to a family, there's a good chance they'll have their own furniture and would therefore prefer unfurnished, but a young professional renting a one-bedroom flat is likely to be looking for somewhere that's already kitted out with a bed, sofa, etc.

If the preference of your target tenant in your local area isn't cut and dried, here are the advantages of each to help you decide...

The case for unfurnished

Letting an unfurnished property is, obviously, much easier for you because you don't have to go to the bother and expense of furnishing it. It also makes life easier throughout the tenancy because if an item of furniture breaks, it will be the tenant's responsibility to fix rather than yours – and at the end of the tenancy there's no potential damage to your furnishings for there to be a disagreement about.

The other advantage is that, in my experience, tenants who move into unfurnished properties tend to stay longer than those in furnished properties. Presumably this is because moving house will be such a pain (once they've bought all their own furniture) that they're in the mindset of staying put unless there's a very good reason to move.

Although you don't want to get into the realms of "part furnished" (because few people are seeking it, and it's unlikely that their "parts" of furniture will be the exact opposite of yours), it's becoming increasingly common to provide a cooker, fridge-freezer and washing machine even in unfurnished properties – as well as the traditional carpets and curtains.

The case for furnished

Personally I don't have a particular problem with furnishing properties. I find that the most common items that need repairing or replacing are washing machines and other white goods, which (as I just mentioned) are often expected to be supplied even in "unfurnished" properties. I'd prefer *not* to furnish, but there's no point in fighting the market: it's better to spend £1,000 on furniture than lose £1,000 in rent because it takes a couple of months to find a tenant.

You can offset the cost of replacing furniture against your tax bill, but it's still better to incur as little cost as possible – so it makes sense economically as well as practically to provide hardwearing furniture in the first place. Despite my reference earlier, Ikea is probably not the answer: it may be cheap, but it's generally not hardy enough to survive more than a couple of years in a rental property. Instead, I tend to use a specialist provider of landlord furniture – which provides furniture that's been specifically chosen to be presentable while also durable and reasonably priced. There are many specialist suppliers around the country, and they also tend to offer "packs" – to save you putting together a shopping list and going to various different shops.

There's a furniture supplier I've used many times who I'd highly recommend. Register your copy of this book at www.property-geek.net/landlord and I'll give you their details.

There isn't an official definition of what "furnished" means, but at the very least tenants would expect the following:

- White goods

- Sofas and a coffee table in the living room

- Beds (with mattresses) and plenty of storage space in the bedrooms (plus desks and chairs if you're renting to students)

I wouldn't personally ever get into the realms of cutlery or small appliances like kettles, which tend to be associated more with holiday lets.

For any furniture you provide (with the exception of curtains and carpets), you *must* ensure that it complies with the Furniture and Furnishings (Fire) (Safety) Regulations 1988. Any modern furniture will comply, but it's worth watching out for if you're buying second-hand (not something I'd recommend) or from abroad.

How to decide

If you're not sure what's most appropriate for your target market, I'd advise calling a local letting agent and just asking hypothetically whether your type of property is more in demand furnished or furnished. (Even though they're not getting any business from me, I find that they don't mind when I do it – or else they mask their annoyance well and take it out on the cat later.)

Alternatively, you can go onto Rightmove and Zoopla and look at the "let agreed" properties like yours to see whether the majority seem to be furnished or unfurnished. Don't look at those that are yet to let: if there are lots of unfurnished properties to let, it's possibly because the furnished ones have already been snapped up!

If you're still in doubt... err on the side of keeping it unfurnished (to start with, at least) and state in your advert (which we'll come to later) that you're flexible. If a few potential tenants

remark that they'd like it to be furnished, then you can do so –
and treat it as a negotiation point so they won't try to knock you
down on the rent.

Chapter 4

Safety requirements

A property that looks good is one thing, but a property that's *safe* is extremely important: while you won't go to prison for having slightly peeling wallpaper, it's a possibility if you don't have a gas safety certificate.

There's no shortage of legislation around the safety aspects of letting a property, but none of it is particularly onerous: the only real risk is that you don't know about your safety responsibilities because no one's ever told you about them. Ignorance is no excuse in the eyes of the law, so it's vital to know your responsibilities – and to stay up-to-date, because legislation is always changing.

In this chapter, I'll help you stay on the right side of the thin blue line by running through all the major safety boxes you need to tick before you let a tenant set foot inside your property.

Energy Performance Certificate

The Energy Performance Certificate (EPC) earns the honour of coming first in this section, because you technically can't even advertise a property for sale or rent until you've got one. You'll also need to give a copy to your tenants when they move in, but I'll remind you about that when we get to that point.

An EPC is issued following an inspection of the property by an accredited assessor, and it gives you a rating of how energy-efficient your home is. A bit of Googling should allow you to easily find an assessor in your area.

From 1st April 2018, you can be fined up to £4,000 for renting out a property that doesn't achieve at least an E on the EPC's A-to-G scale – so if yours comes in lower, you'll need to take some of the recommendations you'll find on the EPC report to bump up the score. (Properties with existing tenancies have until 1st April 2020 to comply – as long as that tenancy doesn't change and a new fixed term isn't agreed with the existing tenant. We'll cover fixed terms and renewals fully in Part 3.)

As you'll see when we come to the section about advertising the property, your advert is legally required to state the numerical rating that appears on the EPC – and if space permits, also the graph showing its rating on the A-to-G scale. This implies that you need to have the EPC done before you can place the advert, but in fact you can market the property for up to 21 days without the EPC rating being displayed as long as you *commissioned* the EPC before the advert went up.

Once issued, an EPC is valid for ten years. This means that if you've recently bought the property, it will have had an EPC done in order for it to be marketed for sale – so you can just reuse the same one (although be sure to check how many years it has remaining). To find out if your property currently has a valid EPC (and to get hold of a copy if you've lost it), all you need to do is visit www.propertygeek.net/epcregister

Gas safety

A far more sensible mandatory document is the landlord's gas safety certificate. A gas safety certificate *must* be obtained every year, and a copy of it *must* be presented to your tenants before they move in – and then again every year when it's renewed.

> *I've put together a checklist of all the major steps involved in letting a property, so register your copy of this book at www.propertygeek.net/landlord and I'll help you make sure you don't forget anything important like a gas safety certificate.*

In order to get a gas safety certificate, all gas appliances in the property (such as the boiler and gas cooker), must be checked by an approved tradesperson who's a member of the Gas Safe Register. There are only two instances in which you don't need a gas safety certificate:

- It's a new build property that's being occupied for the first time. If this is the case, the builder should have issued a document certifying that the installation was inspected before the property was handed over. You'll then need to obtain a gas safety certificate prior to a year from the date that the building was signed off by the inspector (*not* the date that you took ownership).

- There are no gas appliances in the property – e.g. the heating system is communal, there's no boiler, and the cooker is powered by electricity. If there *has* previously been gas supplied to the property but it's no longer needed (e.g. the heating system is communal but you've replaced the gas cooker with an electric one), the gas meter must be removed and the gas supply capped off.

A gas safety certificate can typically cost anything from £40 to £100. Again, it must be renewed annually and a copy supplied to the tenants – so every year, put a reminder in your calendar for a few weeks before your current one expires to give you time to arrange a new one. (You'll need to agree access with the tenant for this, so don't cut it too fine: you won't get any special dispensation if for some reason you weren't able to get hold of them or they weren't willing to give access for a few days.)

Carbon monoxide alarms

It's currently only a legal requirement to fit a carbon monoxide alarm in rooms that constitute living accommodation and also contain an appliance that burns (or is capable of burning) solid fuel, such as wood or coal.

There's currently no legal requirement to fit a carbon monoxide alarm near a boiler – although given that they cost about a fiver, I can't see any reason not to do so anyway.

Electrical safety

As a landlord, it's your responsibility to make sure that the electrical installation of your property is safe when the tenancy begins, and that it remains in proper working order and free of risk throughout the tenancy.

Although an unsafe electrical installation is just as effective a method of accidentally killing your tenants as an unsafe gas installation, it *isn't* currently mandatory (in England and Wales) to hold a particular document.

In a way, this actually makes life more complicated because you still need to be able to prove – in the nightmare scenario that a tenant is injured or has their belongings damaged by an electrical problem – that you've taken all reasonable measures to ensure that the electrics are safe.

So what *should* you do? The Electrical Safety Council recommends that the installation should be tested by a qualified electrician every five years, and you should also make visual checks (for scorching, damaged sockets, exposed wires, etc.) between tenancies and at each inspection.

In addition to taking reasonable steps, it's very important that you're able to *prove* you've done so – which is why any checks (even if only visual checks) you make prior to check-in or during mid-term inspections should be recorded in writing and signed by both you and the tenant.

You might decide, even though it's not currently mandatory, to get a qualified electrician to conduct an Electrical Installation Condition Report (EICR) and renew it every five years. This is already a requirement in Scotland, and the same looks likely to apply in England and Wales soon anyway.

Appliance safety

As well as making sure that the electrical system itself is safe, you're also responsible for assuring the safety of any electrical appliances you provide – like washing machines, fridges, televisions, lawnmowers and so on.

You don't need to check the tenants' own appliances, which is an argument (the first of many we'll see in this book) for having a thorough inventory: in the event of a dispute, it will allow you to prove whether an appliance was provided by you (and is therefore your responsibility) or the tenant.

If you decide to rent the property unfurnished or with just a basic level of furniture like a bed and a sofa, you might have no electrical appliances at all – in which case, no problem. But it's common for even "unfurnished" properties to include white goods like a fridge and washing machine (in modern units they might even be integrated into the kitchen), and these appliances must be safe. (You also, as we'll see later, need to provide the instruction manuals for any appliances.)

There are three things you should consider doing (and keeping a record of) to make sure that supplied appliances are safe:

1. Conduct a visual check of the appliances between each tenancy and during any mid-term inspections to make sure, for example, that cables aren't worn and plugs aren't damaged.

2. Ensure that plugs bear the "CE" mark (which should be present on all newer appliances), which is a statement from the manufacturer that it meets European safety standards.

3. Have a qualified professional conduct a PAT test (that's a Portable Appliance Test test – a syntactical nightmare, but there you go) every two years for smaller items and every four years for larger ones. While this isn't currently a legal requirement in England and Wales (again, it is in Scotland), it's recommended by the Electrical Safety Council.

Fire safety

As we saw earlier when talking about whether to furnish a property, any furnishings that *are* present (except curtains and carpets) need to comply with the Furniture and Furnishings (Fire) (Safety) Regulations (1988). (The people who come up with regulations seem to have a major thing for parentheses.)

It's pretty much impossible to buy furniture in the UK that doesn't comply with these regulations, but it's something to keep in mind if you're buying furniture abroad or second-hand. Look out for a label that specifically mentions the 1988 regulations – otherwise it doesn't comply. Rather than listing out the requirements here, you can find them at propertygeek.net/firesafety

It's worth knowing that the requirements also apply to any furnishings that are on the premises but not accessible to the tenant – so if you have a locked shed or attic that the tenant doesn't have access to, all the furniture stored inside will need to comply with modern regulations too.

Smoke alarms

It's a legal requirement that at least one smoke alarm is fitted on each storey of a property that has any kind of living accommodation – which includes bathrooms and toilets as well as hallways and landings.

The alarm can be of any kind. If you have the choice, hard-wired and interlinked (with a battery backup) is best, but individual battery-powered alarms are perfectly legal too. You just need to make sure that there's an alarm that sounds on every floor – *not* just a sensor.

While it doesn't absolve you of legal responsibility, you should have a clause in the tenancy agreement stating that it's the tenant's responsibility to check the alarms on a regular basis. You should also check the alarms yourself between tenancies and when you conduct periodic visits (which we'll cover later).

Legionella risk assessment

I hadn't heard of legionella until I was setting up Yellow Lettings, and I'd wager that the majority of landlords and letting agents still haven't heard of it.

Nevertheless, as a landlord you have a duty to protect tenants from legionella bacteria – which can be breathed in when it's present in water droplets, and leads to Legionnaires' Disease. The bacteria can grow in domestic water systems like water tanks, pipework and even shower heads.

Much like electrical safety, you don't need any specific certificate but you *can* be fined or imprisoned if a tenant falls ill or dies and you can't prove that you've taken reasonable steps to control the risk. For that reason, it's a smart idea to conduct a Legionella Risk Assessment – and while you can pay someone to do it for you, it's usually an easy task to do yourself.

> *If you want to do your own risk assessment, I'll point you towards a template when you register your copy of this book at www.propertygeek.net/landlord*

It would be a good idea to review the risk assessment whenever something related to the water supply changes (like adding a new en suite bathroom), and issue the guidance sheet to every new set of tenants.

Chapter 5

Insurance

Never has a chapter had a less promising title (although I'll be challenging my own record with one called "How to serve a Section 21 notice" later), so congratulations for your diligence if you're actually reading this.

Insurance bothers me (like it does most right-thinking people) because it's boring and complicated to buy, and then you hope you don't need to use it. If you indeed *do* need to use it, there's a chance that the insurance company will try to wriggle out of actually upholding their side of the bargain. But still, the consequences of *not* having adequate insurance are potentially far worse than having to learn about it – so let's get through this together…

You can insure yourself against pretty much any risk imaginable (for a price), and in this chapter I'll cover the most common types of insurance that a landlord would consider taking out. Sometimes these insurances will be bundled together (a landlord's buildings insurance or contents insurance policy usually includes public liability insurance, for example), but they can also be purchased separately.

For every type of insurance I talk about, there are two important things to keep in mind:

1. It's hugely important to actually read the policy documents and make sure you're covered for what you think you are. You don't want to spend years calmly believing that you're insured against a particular "peril" (as insurers rather dramatically call a specific risk), only to discover when the time comes that you don't have the protection that you thought you did.

2. Tell the full and complete truth about every aspect of the property when you're taking out the policy, and make sure you're not invalidating the policy by failing to maintain your end of the bargain. Again, it would be awful to have your tenant fall downstairs and sue you, only to have your claim rejected because you had a different type of window locks from what was specified in the policy – but this is the kind of thing that can and does happen.

So you can see that it's not a great idea to just go onto a comparison website and pick the cheapest policy without reading it thoroughly: your cheap policy might end up having exclusions and stipulations that render it useless for your intended purpose.

You might decide, especially for cases that aren't entirely

straightforward, to use the services of an insurance broker: you can explain your situation to them in plain English, and they'll go away and find a policy that meets your needs. Because the consequences of being improperly insured can be so serious, I'd very much advise taking the rest of this chapter as the most cursory of inexpert overviews and speaking to a professional.

OK, with that all covered, let's move on to the main types of insurance that you might want to consider.

Buildings insurance

Buildings insurance covers you against damage to the structure of the building itself – that is, anything that you can't take out and move to a different property (those would be covered by contents insurance).

Much like having motor insurance is absolutely essential if you want to drive a car, buildings insurance is a total must if you want to own a property. Unlike motor insurance, it's not a legal requirement – but having proper insurance *will* be a condition of your mortgage if you have any kind of loan against the property.

If your property is a flat within a block, there will typically be a block buildings insurance policy. You'll pay for this as part of your service charge, and you'll receive the policy details each year – at the same time you receive the demand for the service charge to be paid. Your mortgage lender will want to see these policy details, so if you've mislaid them (or are just in the process of buying the property) you can request a copy from the freeholder or their managing agent.

Even if you own the property outright, you still want buildings insurance. Why? Because if you *don't* have it and the property burns down, you have no property and no compensation.

This would be a good time to introduce Rob's Rule For Deciding Whether To Insure Against Something Or Not (which *really* needs a catchier name): if you're not financially and psychologically able to deal with the worst case scenario, insure yourself against it. In the case of the property burning down, you're unlikely to be able to just mentally shrug and write off a loss of hundreds of thousands of pounds, so you need to be insured.

There are several different levels of buildings insurance. The most basic is FLEA, which doesn't actually protect you against infestations – it stands for Fire, Lightning, Explosion and Aircraft. On top of that you can add all sorts of goodies like escape of water, tenant damage (accidental or malicious), terrorism, and plenty more. If you buy a policy specifically intended for landlords (which you should, of course), the buildings policy will often include a limited amount of landlord contents insurance, and cover for alternative accommodation if an insured risk (like fire) makes the property temporarily uninhabitable.

Personally, I always go for at least FLEA plus "escape of water" – making sure that "track and trace" of the leak is included, because digging around to find the source often does more damage than the leak itself.

When taking out insurance, you'll need to know the "rebuild value" to insure for: in other words, if the property were to be completely destroyed, how much would it cost to build it again? This *isn't the same as its market value*: the rebuild value can be either much higher or much lower than what someone would pay for the property, and it's important to get it right so you're not either under-insured or paying for a level of insurance you don't need.

If you've had the property valued recently (for purchase or mortgage purposes), the valuation will state the rebuild value. If you don't have a recent valuation and you don't want to pay for a new one, the Association of British Insurers has a free online calculator – find it at www.propertygeek.net/rebuildvalue. You'll need to know the square footage of the property (which you can take from the EPC), and bear in mind that an online calculation might not be as accurate as a professional's opinion.

As I said in the introduction to this chapter, it's important to read the policy in full and be completely accurate in the inform-ation you provide when taking out the policy. It sounds cynical, but it's true: insurance company employees are sometimes rewarded based on how many claims they deny, so they'll be looking for mistakes you've made in order to avoid paying out.

The most glaring thing you need to tell the insurer is *that the property is being rented out*: it sounds obvious, but it's not at all uncommon for an "accidental landlord" to move out of their home and just keep their old insurance policy going. Beyond that, it's important to be accurate about the type of tenant that occupies the property: if the policy doesn't cover tenants who are on benefits or multiple tenants on individual tenancies, you're not going to get your claims paid out either.

Another clause that's worth looking out for is how the property is treated when it's empty – and what constitutes "empty" for that particular insurer. Take the case of a month's gap between tenants: some insurers will be fine with it, others will want to be notified, and still others will end cover after 14 days. There may also be a requirement to visit the property regularly while it's empty and keep the boiler set to a certain temperature, and insurers also have different opinions on whether a property is considered empty while refurbishment work is going on. Claims are frequently denied when the rules around empty properties haven't been obeyed to the letter, so scour the small print and act accordingly.

> *The company I use for all my buildings insurance promises to beat any like-for-like quote. If you'd like their details, just register your copy of this book at www.propertygeek.net/landlord*

Landlord contents insurance

As I mentioned in the last section, buildings insurance will cover the structure of the building, but not anything that could be dismantled or ripped out and taken away – like carpets, curtains, kitchen units and so on. To cover those, you'll need contents insurance.

Even if you're letting the property unfurnished, there are still likely to be carpets and kitchen appliances – so you might decide that taking out contents insurance is still appropriate. Or then again, given that there's a finite limit to how much it would cost to replace carpets and so on, you might decide that it's a risk you can afford to take and you'll just pay out of pocket if anything happens.

As is becoming a theme here, there are different levels of cover to choose from – including, for example, whether malicious damage by tenants is covered.

The name gives it away somewhat, but it's worth making clear that a landlord's contents insurance policy doesn't cover *tenants'* possessions. You should make your tenants aware of this, and tell them that they might want to consider taking out their own policy to cover their own belongings. It's also another good reason (and we'll see plenty more later) to conduct a thorough inventory at the start of a tenancy, so there's a signed record of which contents are yours if you need to make a claim.

Public liability insurance

Public liability insurance covers you for any ill that befalls a member of the public while on your property – primarily your tenants, but also anyone else who happens to be visiting (and yes, bizarrely you can be sued by a trespasser who injures themselves while breaking into your house).

According to Rob's Rule Of Whatever I Called It Earlier, this is *definitely* a type of insurance that you want – because it's not too hard to imagine a tenant tripping on a loose bit of carpet, falling downstairs and suing you for medical bills, loss of earnings, trauma, and even a lifetime of care bills if they're permanently disabled. You might consider the possibility to be remote, but could you afford to pay a £1m+ claim out of your own pocket if the worst *did* happen? No, me neither.

Public liability insurance is often included when you take out landlord buildings insurance, but you should make sure that's definitely the case – and that the level of cover is adequate. And remember: although being covered for £1m *sounds* like a lot, you might decide that £5m or £10m is more appropriate given how expensive just one catastrophe could be.

As with buildings insurance, insurers will be looking for reasons not to pay out (especially if it's a large claim), so make sure you've done everything required to make a valid claim. A large proportion of claims against landlords, for example, relate to stairs – and many policies aren't valid if you don't have a hand-rail installed.

Rent Guarantee Insurance

I'm a huge fan of Rent Guarantee Insurance (RGI), but landlords are divided on the subject.

The idea is that with an RGI policy, the insurer will take over payments if the tenant defaults on their rent – and will often cover the legal costs of eviction, too. (It's also possible to get policies that cover *only* the legal costs, but not the rent.)

One drawback is that these payments aren't instant: you often (depending on the policy) have to wait until the tenant is a couple of months in arrears, then it takes time to go through the claims process before you actually get the cash.

Another drawback is that insurers are fussy about which tenants they'll guarantee the rent of: they'll want to see the references you've obtained (and sometimes insist on you using their own chosen referencing service), and won't agree to cover tenants with any hint of a chequered credit or payment history.

This gives rise to the totally valid argument that insurers are only willing to provide insurance for tenants who are highly likely to pay anyway – therefore the insurance is an unnecessary cost.

In many ways I agree, and in the long run you're highly likely to come out financially ahead if you don't have the cost of RGI premiums and deal with the odd rent default. But I'd still take it every time.

One reason is that taking out RGI enforces discipline: you can't decide to take a chance on a tenant who doesn't have perfect references, because the insurer wouldn't cover them. But the main reason is that it drastically reduces the maximum amount of time that you could be out of pocket.

For example, say a tenant stops paying rent one month into a 12-month tenancy. Without insurance, it could easily take six months (plus legal fees) to get rid of them – during which time you'd still need to keep paying your mortgage and all other costs. With insurance, you're only out of pocket for a couple of months until the insurance kicks in. As a result, you need a far smaller "emergency fund" in order to weather even the most serious problems a landlord can face.

As with all types of insurance, companies are keen to find any reason not to pay out – so read the policy in minute detail to make sure you follow the claims procedure and don't do anything to invalidate it.

You don't need to make a decision on RGI now, so for now just be aware that it's an option – and read the rest of the book to learn more about the practical and legal aspects of dealing with tenants before choosing what to do.

Conclusion to Part 1

Congratulations: you're officially through the most tedious part of the process! You've obtained consents from all and sundry, got the property into tip-top condition, sorted out the safety requirements and made sure you're insured against all those scary "perils".

We might not have covered the world's most exciting set of topics, but they're important. And now we can safely move onto the good bit: finding the tenants who are going to give you your income...

PART 2:
FINDING TENANTS

Introduction

So, your property is finally ready! You've obtained all the consents, made it look beautiful (but not gone overboard on the gold leaf, of course), conducted all your safety checks and made sure that your insurance is up to scratch. Or if you *haven't* done all of this yet, you've made a list of everything that needs to be readied before a tenant can cross the threshold.

While this book may make it seem like letting a property is a linear process ("get consents, THEN decide on furnishings, THEN call your insurer..."), I'm sure you're aware that real life tends to be messier than that. There's overlap and flexibility everywhere, and "finding tenants" is one area that it's worth starting early: every day that the property is ready but empty is costing you money. There's absolutely no need to wait until, for example, your gas safety certificate is through before you start the process of looking for tenants. Start looking for them *now*.

While some landlords wish it weren't the case, they need tenants if they want to actually make money and stuff. So how do you find them, and – most importantly – how do you find the *right* ones? That's what this section is all about.

At this point it's worth reminding you that throughout this book, I'm assuming that you're opting to do absolutely everything yourself – i.e. without the help of a letting agent.

If you do decide to use an agent, you can choose either a "Let Only" service (which covers everything in Part 2 and Part 3), or a "full management" service (which also covers Part 4 and Part 5). Towards the end of the book, in the first bonus chapter, I'm going to talk about letting agents in more detail, to help you decide if you want to use one or not – but first it's probably best if you at least skim the rest of the book so you know what they're supposed to be doing for you.

The first decision to make when it comes to finding tenants is deciding where to advertise – so that's where we'll begin…

Chapter 6

Where to advertise

If you were looking for a property to rent, where's the first place you'd look? Chances are you just thought "Rightmove" or "Zoopla" – because these are far and away the most popular channels, and therefore the best place for the majority of properties to be marketed.

But there are plenty of other channels too – some of which you might want to add into the mix, and some of which could well be *more* appropriate than the major online portals depending on the type of tenant you want to attract.

The major online portals

It's hardly going to be news that most people's searches for a home to rent now mostly start online – so if you decide to advertise in just once place, you'll probably get the most visibility on portals like Rightmove (www.rightmove.co.uk), Zoopla (www.zoopla.co.uk) and On The Market (www.onthemarket.com). (There are some situations when this isn't the case – and we'll explore those shortly.)

As a private landlord, you can't directly add your property to the main portals yourself, but there are a large number of "online agents" who'll do it on your behalf.

It's a fairly simple process: you usually just provide the online agent with all the necessary information about your property and pay in the region of £50 to £100, then they'll upload the details and photos to the portals and pass tenant enquiries on to you. There will usually be extra services you can add on for an additional fee – like referencing potential tenants, registering the deposit, drawing up the tenancy agreement, and so on.

There are plenty of online agents to choose from, but if you want my recommendation just register your copy of the book at www.-propertygeek.net/landlord

It should go without saying (but clearly doesn't) that your advert needs to be persuasive and effective in order to stand out from the competition on the listings page and actually get viewed – which we'll talk about in the next chapter.

Gumtree

An online resource you *can* upload to directly (although the online agents we just discussed often include it in their service too) is Gumtree (www.gumtree.com) – which currently costs around £25. Gumtree is extremely popular in certain areas (London in particular) and a complete ghost town in others, so – depending on the location of your property – it may or may not be worth your while.

If you decide to give it a go, prepare for some interesting experiences and new insights into the nature of humanity at large. I've no idea why this particularly happens on Gumtree, but applicants who come via the site tend to be (to put it charitably) a mixed bag – so you'll have to invest some time weeding out the nutters, scammers and time-wasters from the few remaining people who you might actually want to occupy your property.

As a general, potentially-offensive-but-nevertheless-accurate rule, Gumtree tends to be more popular with the lower end of the market – both in terms of tenants and quality of properties – so it could be a tool worth using depending on your property and its location, but be aware of its limitations.

Facebook groups

Most towns in the UK have at least one Facebook group for people who are looking for property to rent – just enter the name of the area and a keyword like "rent" into the Facebook search box and you should find relevant groups popping up.

Much like Gumtree, you have nothing to lose except your time... but those time costs can be significant, because (also much like Gumtree) the quality of applicants who are looking for housing on Facebook tends to be more variable than those who are using Rightmove or Zoopla. These groups are particularly popular with tenants on benefits, because they might not be in a position to provide references or pass credit checks and they know that individual landlords are more likely to be flexible than letting agents.

If you do go down the Facebook route, make sure you use the process I outline in a future chapter to minimise the amount of time you spend dealing with applications and viewings.

DSSmove

DSSmove (www.dssmove.co.uk) is "Rightmove for tenants on housing benefit" – with the exceptions that it's free and you *can* add properties directly to DSSmove as a private landlord. If your property type and location are most suited to this sector of the market, it's well worth a try.

Spareroom

If you want to rent out properties by the room, try Spareroom (www.spareroom.co.uk): it generates the most consistent results for people I know who pursue this strategy. It's free but has the opportunity to pay for greater exposure.

University accommodation offices

If you're planning to rent out your property to students, it's worth speaking to the local student accommodation office: they'll usually have their own portal, local advertising and events through which your property can be marketed. Often you'll need to become an "accredited landlord" with the university in order to have them promote your property, which usually involves signing up to some kind of code of practice.

The local paper

As I said at the outset, the channels you use will depend on the demographics of your target tenants. So while the local paper (or indeed other forms of offline marketing like cards in newsagents' windows) might seem outdated, they can be worthwhile if you're trying to appeal to certain sectors of the market – like tenants who are older, or are less likely to have internet access.

Friends and recommendations

If you can have a tenant recommended to you and save yourself the bother of advertising, fantastic – but you *absolutely should not* relax your standards just because they're a friend or you have a friend in common. In fact, I'd be even more diligent about correctly setting up and managing this kind of tenancy, because they might be more likely to take advantage and feel like they could get away with it.

I hope this section has shown you that there are many options for finding tenants – all of which are free or inexpensive – and if your property is in a desirable location and accurately priced (which we'll come to shortly) you won't struggle to find people who are interested in renting from you. So while a recommendation can be a useful thing, don't feel like you need to go with someone you know because you're worried about not being able to find anyone else (because you will) or because you're not confident about "formally" setting up a tenancy (because you still should).

Personally, I wouldn't rent a property to a friend or even a friend-of-a-friend because I like to maintain a separation and not have emotion come into the equation. That doesn't mean you shouldn't – just don't let your guard down.

Chapter 7

How to set the rent

Unless you have a wildly unique property or it's in an area where nothing else is being marketed to let (in which case I'd suggest that it might not be the best rental property in any case), assessing the market rent for a property isn't difficult: you can simply base it on what else is being marketed locally.

There are some special considerations if you're marketing to students, sharers or tenants on benefits (which I'll address specifically at the end of this chapter), but let's start by looking at how to establish the market rent for a property that you're planning to rent as a single unit to working tenants.

Finding rental comparables

Rightmove (or Zoopla, if you prefer – both are similar for this purpose) is the only tool you need to establish the market rent for your type of property. Many other sites and tools profess to spit out "average" rents for an area, but an average by definition misses out too much variation to be useful. The most accurate method is to look at the direct alternatives that potential tenants have, and price your own property accordingly.

So, with Rightmove open:

1.   Enter the postcode of your property and select a search radius of 1/4 mile.

2.   Select the appropriate property type (house or flat) and number of bedrooms.

3.   Select "Include 'Let Agreed' properties".

If only a very small number of properties match your search, you can increase the size of your search area. Rightmove also allows you to draw a search area on the map, which might be appropriate if, for example, your property is right on the edge of the nice part of town – which means a comparable area extends a mile in one direction and not at all in the other.

From the results you're left with, order them by price to make it easier to scroll through and establish the range of rents from lowest to highest. There will usually be one or two outliers that you can ignore (like a fancy penthouse that's way more expensive, or a miscategorised property that's far too cheap), but the rest will fall within a reasonably tight range.

You can then, making every effort to be completely objective, assess where your property "fits" within that range. You'll normally find that rental prices are driven by the following:

•   Location – although if you've chosen a small search area, this won't be so much of a factor

- The square footage, so a two-bedroom property with two reception rooms will command more than a two-bedroom property with a single reception

- (For flats) The type of building (a nice new build will always command more than an ex-local authority block), its age and level of amenities

- (For houses) Whether it's terraced, semi-detached, etc.

- The standard of internal condition

- Whether the property is offered furnished or unfurnished

- Particularly for flats, whether an allocated parking space is provided

- Whether there's a garden, balcony, or any other special features

By looking at the photos, floor plans and descriptions, you can identify the properties most similar to yours and what they're renting for. If the rental market is reasonably active and competitive, you should find that the range from cheapest to most expensive is usually no more than £50 to £75 per month.

Then it's just a case of deciding where you want to position yourself in that range: whether you want to go at the low end to fall within more people's budgets and get more interest quickly, or hold out for a higher level of rent. My advice, unless you're in a mad rush, is to price yourself towards the high end of the range: at Yellow Lettings we find that tenants are generally aware that there's the ability to negotiate, so they'll happily view something that's slightly over their ideal budget. Going near the high end (remembering to stay *within* the range of similar properties) is therefore unlikely to lose you many viewings, and you might get lucky and have someone fall in love with the property who doesn't try to barter you down.

(Useful tip: after you've set your search criteria, set up a Rightmove Alert so that new results get emailed to you every week. This will help you keep an eye on what's happening to prices, standards and trends among your competition – and you'll be better informed next time your property becomes empty.)

> Pro tip: "We find that if someone starts arguing about the price and other comparable properties on the market, it's usually a red flag about a tenant who is going to be difficult. We know our areas and streets really well, and find when potential tenants start comparing properties it won't be like for like – comparing a one-bedroom flat to a two-bedroom terrace, for example. If it really is the case that our property is £100–£300 overpriced, why did they come on the viewing in the first place? There is usually a £50–£100 sweet spot where people just won't consider it overpriced." – Matt Elder

Getting an agent's perspective

Falling into the realm of "morally dubious"... if you're not confident about the comparables you've found on Rightmove, you can always call a local agent pretending to be a tenant, and ask them what kind of rent you could expect to pay for the type of property you're marketing. If you pretend to be a tenant rather than a landlord, the agent has less of a motivation to quote ambitious numbers at you in an attempt to win your business.

Pricing up rooms for sharers

Establishing the rent that you could get for a room in a shared house involves a similar process as for an entire property, but with the exception that you should use Spareroom rather than Rightmove.

When looking at comparables and establishing the range, you also need to bear these things in mind:

- Some prices will include bills and others won't, so make sure you're comparing like with like.

- Some listings will only be for Monday-to-Friday accommodation and will therefore be cheaper.

Finding comparables for room rentals isn't quite as straightforward as with a single property, because the size and quality of the room (and the facilities on offer) vary so much more. With time, however, you'll start to develop an eye for what's what.

Setting rents for tenants on benefits

If you're targeting a property at tenants who receive housing benefit, you can use Rightmove in the same way as before to assess comparables – and use the same method on DSSmove, too.

It's also useful to be aware of the level of Local Housing Allowance (LHA) that your potential tenants are entitled to, because this will be an important factor in what they can afford – although as benefits caps and Universal Credit are coming into effect, working out what they can afford towards housing is becoming less clear-cut.

You can enter your property's postcode and see the level of LHA that is currently being paid at www.propertygeek.net/lha

You can, of course, target tenants on benefits and charge a rent *higher* than the amount of money they get towards their housing costs – which means that the tenants would need to pay a top-up from their other income. It's just a case of whether you want to maximise the rent at the possible cost of having tenants struggle and fall into arrears, or whether you'd prefer a lower rent and potentially easier life.

Chapter 8

How to write a great advert

Once you've set a sensible level of rent and decided where to advertise, it's time to write the advert that will send your phone into meltdown with people calling to book viewings.

It doesn't need the creativity of an Apple campaign or a Ronseal-esque slogan that will be tripping off people's lips for years to come: it just needs to positively but honestly describe the property, and give people the information they need to decide whether to spend time viewing it. If a critical piece of information is lacking (such as the date the property is available from), they'll only bother to enquire if they've fallen hopelessly in love with it: it's far more likely they'll just move on to the next one in the list.

So in this chapter, we'll run through all the information you should be including in your advert – and how to present it in a way that attracts your ideal tenants.

The rent

Unsurprisingly, rent is the main thing potential tenants will want to know – so include this prominently, and follow the norms of your local target market as to whether you state the rent in terms of the weekly or monthly amount. (And this might sound daft, but there are landlords who don't realise that there are more than four weeks in a month – you need to multiply weekly rent by 4.33 to arrive at the monthly rent.)

If anything else is included in the rent (like council tax or utility bills), make sure you say so too.

When the property is available

If the property isn't available immediately, state when it is – to avoid wasting the time of people who need to move right away.

Also state if you're specifically looking for short lets (normally classified as less than six months).

Whether it's furnished or unfurnished

Another option is "part-furnished", but, as I explained earlier, this is best avoided if possible: it's unlikely that your parts of furniture will mesh perfectly with theirs.

Some unfurnished properties come with appliances like washing machines and others don't, so make sure this is clear in your advert.

If the property is unfurnished but you don't object to providing furniture, you can always list it as being "flexible". This is a nice option because it means you won't be shelling out for furniture when you might not need to, but it also won't put off tenants who are looking specifically for furnished accommodation.

Fees payable by tenants

It's a legal requirement that your advert states any fees that a potential tenant will be expected to pay.

This includes the "application fee" or "admin fee" that you might decide to charge to cover the cost of gathering references and setting up the tenancy, as well as the deposit that the tenant will be required to pay. (Rules about the fees you can charge seem likely to be changing soon – which I'll explain in more detail later.)

We'll look at what is reasonable to charge in terms of these fees in a later chapter – but for now, just be aware that they must be stated in your advert.

Requirements for the tenants you'll accept

It's against the law to discriminate on the grounds of race, religion, gender, age, sexual orientation, marriage and disability when it comes to who you'll rent to – but you may have some other stipulations that are worth stating in the advert.

The most common are "No DSS" (now known as Local Housing Allowance, but the old term "DSS" is still commonly used by almost everyone – including the recipients) and "No pets".

Whether you choose to make these stipulations in the advert

(rather than just decide case-by-case) is up to you. The argument for doing so is that if you're very unlikely to accept certain people, you'll save everyone time by saying so and not having unsuitable people apply. However, it's very hard for LHA claimants and pet owners to find suitable rented accommodation – so by being open-minded you'll open yourself up to a large part of the market who don't have many other options.

You may well take the view that while there are some shocking LHA tenants, there are some shocking professional tenants too – and that while you might not want a Doberman in your house, you wouldn't object to a hamster. By not stating a preference, you can find out people's exact circumstances when they apply and make a decision based on the facts.

It's also a good idea to let tenants know what information you'll require from them in order to check their references (which I'll talk about in a future chapter). This will stop some (but not all) tenants who can't provide this information from wasting your time – and gives the message that you know what you're doing and won't allow any chancers to pull the wool over your eyes.

Photos

Photos – *good* photos – are the most important part of any property advert, with between 6 and 12 being the optimum number depending on the size of the property.

To understand why photos are so important, think back to when you last bought or rented a property. When you're browsing through hundreds of search results, you'll only click on the ones that look appealing – and then you need to be sufficiently tempted to pick up the phone and commit half an hour of your life to going to view it.

To give your listing the edge, I'd say it's well worth investing in professional photography. "Professional" doesn't have to mean "expensive": I've had photos done for £60–£100 by friends of friends or photographers I've found on Gumtree. And remember, you can reuse the photographs every time the property becomes available (as long as nothing has significantly changed), so this is only a one-off expense.

If you're providing some level of furnishing, it's a good idea to "stage" the property if at all possible – artfully placed flowers, cushions and steaming cups of coffee will help the viewer imagine what it's like to live there, and will help it stand out even further from the other listings.

Even if you don't stage the property to the extent that it looks like it's come straight out of Swanky Interiors magazine, *please* avoid the cardinal sins of property photography: bare lightbulbs, unmade beds (or beds with no bedding), toilets with the lid up, closed curtains, mess.

All listings sites will allow you to choose the "lead" photograph, which is displayed in the main search results page. Make this photo your best one – the one that will jump out from a page of listings and look the most desirable. While there's no harm at all in including an exterior shot, lead with internal photos: unlike buyers who are looking to some extent for an investment, it's lifestyle that matters to renters.

Pro tip: "I include a walkaround video of every property (made when the property has just been cleaned) and include that in my listing on Rightmove, etc. It gives potential tenants a much better idea of the property." –Kylie Ackers

Floor plan

A floor plan can be extremely helpful, especially if your property is a studio (a term that can encompass everything from "box room with a sink" to "giant warehouse which happens not to have a separate bedroom") or a house (where layout matters a lot to families). It's less important for a one- or two-bedroom flat because the layout tends to be quite standard, but it's still nice for the viewer to be able to piece together the photos in their mind.

Again, a floor plan is a one-off cost that could make the difference between your dream tenant picking up the phone or clicking away because they can't tell if the property will be suitable for them. If you don't want to pay for one to be drawn up, search "floor plan app" and you'll discover multiple apps for iPhone and Android that help you to do it yourself.

Property description

This is where I expressly ban you from using awful property clichés. Instead, stick to the important facts and write them in a way that's clear for someone to quickly browse and extract the information they need.

You'll want to include:

- The type of property – house, flat, maisonette and so on

- Whether it's terraced, semi-detached or detached (if it's a house)

- Which floor it's on and whether it's part of a converted house or purpose-built block (if it's a flat or maisonette)

- The number of bedrooms, and whether they're singles or doubles (bear in mind that if a loft room is used as a bedroom, it can only be *described* as a bedroom if the conversion has Building Control approval)

- The number of bathrooms (and whether or not they're en suite), and whether there's a shower, a bath, or both

- The number of reception rooms, and a description of each

- What's included in terms of furnishings (if any)

- Which appliances are included in the kitchen

- Whether there's any kind of outdoor space, like a balcony or garden

- Any kind of parking arrangements, such as if there's a

driveway or allocated on- or off-street parking

On top of this, you can describe any positive features of the property – such as if it's been recently refurbished, has unique or original features, is in a particularly quiet location, and so on.

And the negative features? No property is perfect, but most imperfections aren't deal-breakers if there are enough positive features to excite the tenant. I'd say that it's worth mentioning in passing any negatives that *are* likely to be make-or-break for a significant number of tenants – like if it's opposite a pub or in a high-rise in the middle of a council estate – because otherwise you're just wasting your time in taking viewings.

Area description

You can't assume that potential tenants will be familiar with the exact location of your property, so it's a good idea to include a brief description of the area. You can tailor this to your likely target market – so talk about schools and safety if you're expecting to rent to a family, and nightlife and transport if you're targeting young professionals or students.

In general, look to include:

- Transport links, including distance from major bus, train and road links

- Parks, open spaces and any landmarks of particular interest

- The proximity of shopping centres and supermarkets

When it comes to written descriptions in general, don't be daunted and get flashbacks to writing essays at school – just think about what you'd want to know if you were potentially renting your property, and write it down in straightforward language. If you're particularly uncomfortable writing, you might find it helpful to record the description first, then listen back and type it out. However you do it, it's worth getting someone to check it over for typos and missed information before you put it live: you'll always make some kind of mistake first time.

Energy performance rating

As I mentioned in Part 1, it's a legal requirement that an EPC is commissioned before a property is advertised. The advert itself should contain the numerical rating from the certificate, and the guidance notes state that it's advisable to include a copy of the A-to-G graph from the certificate where space permits.

As I also mentioned, once the EPC has been commissioned you have a 21-day window to get the results – so you can in fact advertise the property without the EPC score initially, then add it in later.

Chapter 9

Fees

Earlier I said that your property advert should mention any fees that potential tenants will need to pay. So what are those fees, exactly?

Holding deposit

It's not acceptable to charge a fee for showing a property to a potential tenant, but you might decide to take a holding deposit once they've viewed the place and they definitely want to move in.

For the tenant, a holding deposit gives them the reassurance that you won't move ahead with any other applicants while you go through the referencing process with them.

For you, it's a disincentive for the tenant to pull out at the 11th hour after wasting weeks of your time: if they decide during the process that a better option has come along and they don't want to move in after all (or if they fail referencing checks), they forfeit their deposit and you've got some compensation for your wasted effort.

The amount of the holding deposit can be anything – you might decide on a week's rent or a couple of hundred pounds. When you receive it, issue the applicant with a receipt that states what the money is for, under what conditions it might be returned (normally just if you, the landlord, pull out), and what will happen to it when the tenancy begins (normally it becomes part of the first month's rent). Ideally, get the tenant to sign this receipt so there can be no confusion claimed later.

Importantly, the holding deposit is entirely separate from a damage deposit – with the latter needing to be treated in a very specific way by law. We'll cover that later, so for now, just know that they're completely different things even though they share the word "deposit".

Referencing fees

At the time of writing, the government is consulting on a proposal to ban charging upfront fees to tenants. If the ban actually happens, it seems that it'll only apply to letting agents rather than private landlords – but do keep an eye out for more details, because the consultation is likely to end before this book gets its next update. Joining my mailing list at www.propertygeek.net is an excellent way of staying updated on this and all other property issues.

So… as of right now, you as a private landlord can still choose to charge tenants a referencing fee. You could keep this fee low to just cover your true out-of-pocket costs of referencing, or higher to compensate you for your time, too. I think £50 per adult occupier is perfectly reasonable – but there's no reason not to charge more if you think the market will bear it, or charge no fee at all as a selling point.

What happens to referencing fees if the tenancy doesn't go ahead for some reason? As a rule:

- If the tenant pulls out after referencing costs have been incurred, the fees they've paid are non-refundable.

- If you as the landlord pull out for any reason other than the tenant failing referencing checks (for example, you decide not to rent the property out after all), you return the tenant's fees in full.

- If the tenant fails referencing checks, you return any fees they've paid *after* you've deducted the *actual* cost you've paid for the referencing.

Damage deposit

The deposit, "damage deposit" or "bond" (all the same thing) is the amount of money that the tenant pays you in order to protect you against any damage or unpaid bills at the end of the tenancy. As I explained earlier, your property advert should state how much deposit you'll require.

(When you receive a deposit, you'll need to register it with a government-approved scheme; we'll cover this next.)

A typical deposit is six weeks' rent. Why six weeks rather than a month? Because it's not uncommon for tenants to skip the last month's rent on the grounds that "they've got my deposit anyway" (even though this isn't allowed). By keeping a deposit equal to six weeks' rent, it ensures you still have some money left over to cover damage or unpaid bills even if the last month's rent isn't paid. This isn't set in stone, though: you can decide to lower the deposit requirement to one month, raise it to two months, or do pretty much whatever you like.

You can also choose not to ask for a deposit at all, and instead take out a specialist insurance product – often called No Deposit Insurance (fittingly enough) – which will pay out against any damage that would normally be covered by a deposit. You can pass the (relatively small) cost of the insurance premium on to the tenant in return for not asking for a deposit.

There are good arguments for going down the insurance route:

- It's obviously more attractive to tenants, who don't need to find a large sum of money – particularly if they're moving between rental properties and need to pay the deposit for your property before they're received the deposit back from their last property.

- As such, it's a selling point that might see your property let faster.

- It saves the hassle and paperwork of registering it with a government scheme.

- There won't be any disputes about deductions from the deposit at the end of the tenancy.

Despite these advantages, I would personally still take a deposit rather than go down the insurance route. Why? There's a lot to be said for tenants having skin in the game: they're likely to take better care of the property if they have their deposit at stake, rather than if they know someone else will pick up the bill. Even though in theory you'll get paid back for the damage either way, it's still preferable to avoid the inconvenience of getting repairs done – and you're unlikely to recover the full cost of the repair in any case.

Chapter 10

Conducting viewings

Conducting viewings can involve a fair bit of hard work and running around, but look at it this way: it's a lot better than *not* having viewings, because it means you're potentially just one short conversation (and a lot of dull paperwork) away from successfully letting out your property.

Viewings are an area that can easily take over your life for a couple of weeks if you let them – but they don't have to. Follow the tips in this chapter and you'll glide through the process of finding your perfect tenant with supreme efficiency.

Fielding phone calls

Depending on how you've advertised your property, you'll be receiving either emails or phone calls from potential tenants. (Or if you used an advertising platform, you'll be getting messages about potential tenants you need to call back.)

Around two-thirds of all the enquiries you get will come in the first 48 hours, because potential tenants will often have alerts set up for when new properties are listed. If you've got a particularly busy couple of days coming up, wait before you put the advert live – or have someone lined up to step in for you.

You'll need to speak to these potential tenants in order to qualify them (and set up a viewing, if they seem suitable) as quickly as possible. Time is of the essence because people normally want to find somewhere to rent as soon as possible – but even so, it's not particularly efficient to be receiving calls and messages all day when you might be at work.

There are a couple of methods you can use to deal with phone calls in particular:

- Buy a pay-as-you-go SIM card or Skype number to put on the advert, leave the phone off and just check messages once per day so you can call everyone back in one go.

- Sign up to a call answering service (I've used www.answer.co.uk, but many others are available) and get them to take a message and email you with details of who you need to call back – so again, you can get back to them all in one batch.

If you're worried about safety, another advantage of both these methods is that you don't have to give out your real phone number, and you can just withhold your number when you call back.

Qualifying potential tenants

You might like to think people will read your comprehensive advert in detail and make sure it's suitable before they call you for a viewing... but that's never going to happen. However clearly you state that it's a top-floor flat for £500 per month and you don't accept pets, you *will* receive calls from people asking if there's room in the garden for their dogs to exercise and if their £300 budget will be acceptable to you.

So to avoid wasting everyone's time, it's best to get on the phone and ask some questions – ideally using a checklist so you ask everyone for the same information and don't forget anything:

- When do they want to move? This may or may not fit in with the date your property is available. If somebody wants to move *right now*, do a bit of digging and find out why: be wary if they seem too desperate, and especially if they offer unprompted to pay all the rent upfront.

- Where are they living now, and why are they moving? Acceptable answers will depend on your tolerance for drama, but I'd consider it a red flag to get any kind of sob story or rant about their current landlord at this point. People do have terrible experiences, of course, but I'd want a tenant to be smart enough to keep it short and to the point.

- Do they meet the requirements you set out? It's not easy to tactfully ask if they have references and a job (if that's what you're requesting), but it needs to be done. It's not uncommon for tenants to be vague about things like this and only disclose after the viewing that they depend on benefits – perhaps because they think you'll be psychologically committed at this point.

- Is the property suitable for them? Make sure they've read the advert properly and know the basics about the number of bedrooms, the rent, and so on. Remember: they'll probably be speaking to a lot of people about a lot of properties, and it's easy to get confused and book a viewing for the "wrong" property.

It'll take some practice to build rapport and give them a chance to ask questions without being stuck on the phone for hours, but after a few goes at it you'll have mastered the art. Ideally within five minutes, you'll have established whether the property is suitable for them, whether they're suitable for *you*, and if you have a gut feel that they're decent people.

Can you rely on gut feel? Not on its own as enough to say "yes": you need to thoroughly reference any applicant, which we'll discuss in the next chapter. But there's nothing wrong with getting a funny feeling about someone and using it as a reason to say "no". If you've got no easy-to-explain reason to turn them down but you want to anyway, a tactful way to extract yourself is to say you have a viewing booked shortly and you'll let them know, then call back later to say that your earlier viewer made an offer on the property – which you've accepted.

Pro tip: "Your gut feel is usually right: if you wouldn't want someone round for tea, don't let your property to them. When I let to students, I ask myself if this is the kind of person I'd want my children to be friends with. When I go against this, it always proves to be the wrong move." –Jeremy Startup

Booking in the viewings

If you do decide to offer a viewing to a particular applicant, I strongly recommend that you offer them a few specific time slots over the coming week – and if someone can't make any of them, so be it. You don't want to spend your life shuttling back and forth for viewings (especially if you live a fair distance away) – and if you make a special trip for just one viewing, sod's law dictates that it'll be *that* person who doesn't show up.

When arranging viewing times, also bear in mind that if a tenant is already living there, you'll need to give them at least 24 hours' written notice of your intention to visit – which they're free to refuse. In this situation it might be a good idea to agree block viewing times with your tenants before putting the advert live, so that you don't have to potentially mess viewers around by changing times if your tenants refuse access.

Perhaps offer a couple of evenings and a weekend session, and give the applicant a 15-minute slot within one of those. In practice, some of your viewings will overlap due to latecomers and people arriving early, but I don't consider that a bad thing: it stokes up demand if two people are looking at once, or if someone's arriving just as another is leaving.

The drawback is that it's hard to have a detailed chat with a serious applicant if someone else is just turning up, so you could consider taking a partner or friend in order to conduct two viewings at once if necessary. You might want to do this for safety anyway.

After you've confirmed the viewing time, take a mobile number and text them with a pre-written template that includes the exact address and directions if it's tricky to find. That way they've got your number and all the relevant details to refer back to.

> Pro tip: "It's much easier to cut and paste templates using software that lets you send SMS messages though a desktop web browser – Mightytext (www.mightytext.net) is a good option for Android phones. You can also have templates to use during the tenancy, like confirming inspection times." –Matt Elder

The viewing itself

If the property being viewed is tenanted, bear in mind that you're required to give the current tenants 24 hours' advance written notice (which can be a text or email) of your intention to visit the property. If they refuse, you must abide by their wishes. This is why it's important to stay on good terms with tenants after they've given their notice to leave (which I'll discuss in a future section), because if they won't cooperate with viewings (in terms of allowing access and making sure the property doesn't look like a scene from Trainspotting), you'll have no choice but to wait until they move out before you hold viewings – leading to void periods.

On the day itself, you might want to consider texting the people who are lined up to view and asking them to confirm that they're coming: while one no-show out of an evening block of ten viewings wouldn't be too dire, it's not beyond the realms of possibility that every one of them realises England are playing that night and they all need to cancel.

Whether the property is empty or tenanted, try to get there a little early to tidy up, turn up the heating if it's winter, open the windows to let in some fresh air if it's summer, and generally make sure the place gives the best possible first impression when someone walks through the door. If you want to take it a step further and bake some bread or bring some fresh flowers, go right ahead.

When viewers arrive, be prepared to answer basic questions about the property. Not everyone is confident in knowing what questions to ask, though, so volunteer the information that seems relevant to them too:

- Any particularly noteworthy features of the property and/or development (they'll guess that the room with the cooker is the kitchen, but might not spot the understairs storage or know that there's a 24-hour concierge)

- Where the nearest station, bus stop, convenience store

and supermarket are

- The parking situation

- How much the council tax and energy bills cost

It's also a legal requirement to have that pesky EPC available at the property, in case anyone wants to see it. In practice I'd say it's acceptable to show it to them on your phone and offer to email a copy (and who on earth asks to see an EPC anyway?), but it might be helpful to print off a copy of the property listing (including the EPC rating) along with your contact details for them to take away.

If someone is making positive noises, you could also expand on the questions you were asking over the phone (in the guise of casual conversation):

- Will anyone else – other than the people viewing – be living with them?

- Where do they work, and how long have they worked there?

- Where are they living at the moment, and why are they moving?

If they seem to be asking a lot of questions and sticking around, chances are they're keen – and if you don't receive an expression of interest from them at the time or later that evening, it's worth following up with them the next day.

However, be on alert for anyone who seems *too* keen – especially if they offer you cash there and then at the viewing, or soon after. There's likely to be something funny going on, or they might just be impulsive and disorganised. Either way, it's not something you want to be dealing with, however keen you are to have someone move in quickly.

Taking offers

When you receive an offer, you don't have to accept it: if you don't get a good vibe from the person or their circumstances seem dubious, just tell them you've already accepted another offer and move on.

If you're interested but the potential tenant has offered a lower rent than you were originally asking for, the ball is entirely in your court. You can:

- Stick to your guns if you're confident of getting a full offer

- Meet in the middle

- Find another negotiating point (like full rent but you'll provide some extra furniture that they don't have)

- Accept their lower offer

It's up to you. Just remember: if you reject an offer that's lower by £25 per month and it takes you another month to find someone to pay full price, you'll need over a year to recoup the rent you missed out on while the property was empty.

Once you're happy with a potential tenant's offer, talk through what will happen next and what's required of them:

1. Confirm that their expectation of when they can move in fits with when the property will be ready for them.

2. Confirm that they're happy to sign a tenancy agreement for the length of time you're looking for (normally 6 or 12 months, possibly with a break clause).

3. Remind them of any holding deposit that you said was necessary to stop showing the property, under what circumstances they'll receive some or all of it back, and where they should pay it to.

4. Clarify what remaining deposit will need to be paid before they move in.

5. Run through what documentation they'll be asked for as part of the referencing process.

Putting this in writing would be a good idea: it makes sure there's no confusion about what's expected from each side and shows that you're a good landlord who's taking this seriously. It'll also make it less likely that they'll continue with the application if they know they'll need to provide something that exposes any fibs they made previously about their circumstances.

> *Pro tip: "When a property is let, spend £25 on an 'arrival kit': a big plastic storage box ready for the day your new tenants move in. In mine, I put toilet rolls, tea, coffee, biscuits, washing-up liquid, toilet cleaner, hand soap, a couple of bottles of wine and a bar of chocolate. It puts you on good terms with the tenant from day one." –Adrian Bond*

With all this agreed and the holding deposit (if any) banked, it's time to start the referencing process…

Chapter 11

Referencing potential tenants

Here's one simple rule that will make your landlording life about a million times easier: *don't scrimp on running background checks on your tenants*. However firm their handshake, charming their manner or desperate you are to get the property filled, referencing is something worth getting right – because the only thing worse than no tenant is a bad tenant.

Getting proof of ID

Your first task is to ascertain that the tenant really is who they say they are – and you can accomplish this by looking at their passport or photocard driving licence (originals, not copies). You should make a copy – either by taking a photo on your phone (which is the easy, sensible method) or going off in search of a photocopier (which is why no one should ever be nostalgic about the old days).

Establishing the Right To Rent

If you've ever fancied a career in border security, good news: you can add that to the list of roles you now have to carry out as a landlord.

The only downside is that – unlike a normal border security guard – you won't get paid. Oh, and you'll be fined and possibly imprisoned if you don't do your job properly.

This requirement is known as a "Right To Rent" check, and it means you need to establish that every adult who'll be living in the property (as their main home) is eligible to reside in the UK. You have to perform this check for every potential tenant, as it's also illegal to only check people who you suspect aren't British citizens.

The Right To Rent check involves seeing each person's original residence documents (such as a residence permit, work visa or Certificate of Entitlement to the right of abode in the UK) while you're face-to-face with them, and satisfying yourself that they're genuine and that the dates haven't expired. You should make a copy, and keep that copy for a year after they stop being your tenants.

If their permission to stay in the UK is time-limited, you also need to make follow-up checks either every 12 months or (if the time limit has less than a year remaining) just before the tenant's right to stay is due to expire.

Using a referencing provider

Once you've established that the tenant is who they say they are and that they have the right to be in the UK, you're off to a strong start. Unfortunately, you still don't have enough information to be confident that they can rent your property. You'll also want to check that they're earning enough to afford the rent, that they don't have a chequered credit history, and (if possible) that previous landlords were happy with their behaviour.

While you could collate all the necessary bits of paper and make the calls yourself, I recommend using one of the many referencing companies out there instead. After all, why spend two days chasing around when you could get it done by someone else for £25?

However, some landlords prefer to spend the time and go into detail themselves – personally going through bank statements and speaking to referees to make absolutely sure the tenant is the right kind of person. There's nothing wrong with taking this approach either, as long as you've got the time to spare to do it properly.

> *Pro tip: "Credit files tell you little. Bank statements and pay slips tell you a lot." –Brian Smart*

If you go down the route of using a referencing company, most of them work the same way: you provide the tenant's name and contact details to the company, and they (normally) email the tenant to get all the information they need. Using that information, they'll then contact all relevant third parties to run the checks, and finally email you a report with their findings.

If everyone concerned is on the ball, this could all be done in a couple of days – but if the tenant or a referee drags things out, it might end up taking longer.

The information collected by referencing companies will vary by company and by the packages they offer. If I were you, I'd shell out for the most comprehensive option – which will normally include:

- A check to see if they have any county court judgments (CCJs) against them

- A bankruptcy and insolvency check

- Any undisclosed previous addresses, and any credit linked to their past addresses (because if they're not telling you about a past address, is that because they didn't behave brilliantly there?)

- Confirmation that they're allowed to reside in the UK (although this doesn't remove the requirement for you to do your own checks: the Right To Rent law requires that you see the original documents, whereas the referencing provider won't)

- An electoral roll check to see if they can be found at the previous addresses listed

- Verification that the bank account details provided genuinely belong to them

- A reference from their current or previous landlord

- Verification of their employment status and income from their employer

A good referencing provider will be able to adjust the information they request to effectively reference potential tenants of any status – including corporate tenants, students, people who are self-employed, people who are retired, and so on.

If the references come back and everything is glowing, great! While there are no guarantees (because a professional tenant with impeccable credit history could suffer from a major life event and go hopelessly off the rails tomorrow), a good gut feel *plus* a good set of references goes a long way towards indicating that this is someone you want living in your property.

But, of course, the references might *not* be so good…

What if the references aren't satisfactory?

If you've been clear from the very start about what you'll be checking and the documents you'll require, anyone trying to do some wool-pulling will (with any luck) give up before reaching the referencing stage. But still, there's always a chance that the references will come back and throw up a nasty surprise. What then?

Let's imagine they've said they're on a permanent contract, but you discover it actually ends in six months. Or they've told you they're currently living with parents, whereas actually they're renting from a landlord who might not give them a positive reference. Or they've shown you anything else in the past that turns out not to be true... what should you make of it?

If I were you, I'd consider that a huge red flag. Innocent mistakes and crossed wires happen, but I wouldn't personally take a risk on someone who appeared to be dishonest from the start.

But then there are times when, through no fault of the tenant's, it's just not possible to gather sufficient data: maybe they've only just graduated, or they're new to the UK (but here legally) and don't have any credit history. You might also be dealing with a self-employed applicant whose business is doing very well, but they're paying themselves a wage that's too low (on paper) to afford the rent. In situations like these, you have a few options:

- If you're in a position to be picky, reject them in favour of someone you can be more sure about.

- Accept them, but only on a six-month tenancy with the entire rent paid upfront. If after six months they want to stay and would pass your reference checks by this point, you can move to a normal arrangement – otherwise they can just pay the next six months upfront again.

- Ask for a guarantor (more on this next).

Asking for a guarantor

A guarantor is someone who co-signs the tenancy agreement

with the tenant and becomes legally liable for the rent if the tenant doesn't pay up. They're also responsible for any damage caused in excess of the deposit. Normally, you'd only ask for a guarantor if the tenant has failed referencing or you know in advance that they *will* fail because (for example) they don't have sufficient income.

Ideally the guarantor will own their own home, because it means they're likely to have assets you can pursue them for if necessary. On a less legal level, it also means they have something to lose and will keep on top of the tenant to make sure they don't get behind on their payments.

You should reference check the guarantor in the same way as you did the potential tenant, and it's not unreasonable to ask the tenant to pay for your costs of doing so.

In situations where there are two or more unrelated tenants, make sure that the guarantor is clear about what proportion of the rent they're guaranteeing. Where you have two or more sharers on the same contract, they are typically "jointly and severally liable" – meaning that if the rent isn't paid, you can pursue either one of them for the full amount owed. You'd normally want any guarantor to similarly have liability for the entire rent (because if some of the rent doesn't show up, it's tricky to prove *whose* rent didn't show up), so make sure they understand this. If you have multiple tenants on separate tenancy agreements, then each tenant who doesn't pass referencing would need their own guarantor to cover just their own part of the rent.

Referencing tenants on benefits

It's somewhat tricky to reference people who are receiving housing benefit: circumstances vary, of course, but it's not uncommon to come across potential tenants who have no employer, no past landlords, and either a bad or non-existent credit history. Someone with these circumstances could be a model tenant, but could also be an absolute disaster waiting to happen.

In speaking to people who are experienced in dealing with housing benefit tenants, I've found that many of them don't bother with reference checks at all: they know they'd fail them anyway, and they're willing to use their gut feel after questioning the potential tenant to determine whether to accept them. They will often try to meet potential tenants at their *current* home, because however well they talk the talk, seeing how well they treat the place they live now will be the best predictor of how they will act in future.

The key thing here is that these landlords are *experienced* in dealing with this type of tenant: not only are they going to be better able than the average person to sniff out the signs of unreliability, but they'll also have a portfolio that wouldn't be catastrophically affected by one or two tenants not paying their rent.

I'd recommend doing at least a basic reference check on *any* tenant to establish that they are who they say they are, that they're allowed to be in the UK, and that the story they've told you (about their past addresses, for example) is consistent with reality.

You can also insist on a guarantor, just like you would for any other tenant who doesn't pass referencing checks. This is helpful because it shows that the potential tenant has some kind of support network, it means someone else other than you will have a vested interest in them paying their rent, and it will allow you to get Rent Guarantee Insurance from some providers.

Conclusion to Part 2

We've covered a lot of ground in this section: we've chosen where to market the property, set the level of rent, written a killer advert, established the fees, done the viewings, and referenced the potential tenants who want to live in the property. Phew!

It's been a huge amount of work, but as a result you've picked a great tenant who'll make your life dramatically easier for the months or years until they move out. You'll never know how much easier, in fact, until you've picked a *bad* tenant and found out how much work that can be.

You can't sit back just yet, I'm afraid: the process of setting up the tenancy correctly is another area that you *must* get right to save yourself from nasty complications further down the line. That's what we'll devote our attention to in the next section – and the good news is that it's a simple matter of correctly following the process I set out. No luck or judgement is involved whatsoever.

PART 3:
SETTING UP THE TENANCY

Introduction

After a lot of hard work, your property is ready and the tenants have been found. Now all that stands between you and your new social pariah status as a "greedy landlord" is… a big pile of pretty dull paperwork.

Doing pre-tenancy admin won't be a thrill-a-minute part of your life that you'll look back on misty-eyed in your later years, but it *is* fundamental to everything that follows – which is why it gets a whole section of its own.

This is the most "procedural" part of the book: there's a lot of tedious background information you need to know about tenancy agreements, followed by steps you need to follow in order. But it's arguably the most important: setting up the tenancy on the right footing is critical to everything that follows.

Plus, by the end of this section you'll have rent in your bank account – so let's get on with it!

Chapter 12

All about tenancy agreements

You'll know what a landlord is, and what a tenant is, and that a "tenancy" exists between the two. But you probably haven't given much thought to what a tenancy really *means*.

Under a tenancy, you grant the tenant a set of rights to a property for a period of time: rights that supersede your own. For example, you give up your right to occupy the property, and the tenant has that right instead – and now you can only visit the property with their permission. Once the tenancy is created, it can only be undone by following a specific legal process.

Because of the way UK law works, a tenancy is automatically created – whether you like it or not – when somebody occupies a property and pays rent. You might think that you can verbally agree to let someone move in for a month, then call the police if they refuse to leave, but no: they now have an (unwritten) tenancy and you'll have to go to court to get them out. The tenancy that's been created is governed by the Housing Act 1988 – a piece of law you'll come to be more familiar with than you might have hoped.

Having an automatically created tenancy with no written documentation to back it up isn't a good situation to be in. The tenant has certain rights, and you have some rights too... but there's no written record of how long the tenancy is intended to last for, how much rent will be paid, or anything else that's been agreed between you. In the event of any dispute, it will be very hard to get the courts to help you because it's your word against theirs.

That's where the tenancy agreement comes in. A well-written agreement is both a legal document and a "user manual" that specifies how the landlord/tenant relationship will work. When any situation arises during the tenancy – as major as the tenant wanting to leave, or as minor as them wanting to put up a poster in their bedroom – you can turn to the tenancy agreement to see what should be done.

Within a tenancy agreement you can include almost anything you like, but it *can't* contradict the rights that each party would have under housing law even if no document existed. Think of the tenancy agreement as an extra layer built on top of housing law that provides more detail, rather than replacing it in any way.

What is an Assured Shorthold Tenancy?

The default type of tenancy in England and Wales is known as an Assured Shorthold Tenancy (AST). An AST is what comes into existence even if no written agreement exists at all.

(In Scotland, this isn't the case. You can read more about the types of tenancy in Scotland in the bonus chapter at the end.)

Other types of tenancy exist, but they're not as landlord-friendly and you have to deliberately override the default to create one – so the vast majority of new tenancies in England and Wales are ASTs. For that reason, the terms "tenancy agreement" and "AST" tend to be used interchangeably among landlords and letting agents. For the rest of this book I'll tend to say "tenancy agreement" when I'm talking about the document you draw up, but you'll know that if you ever see "AST" elsewhere it will mean the same thing.

When is a tenancy not an AST?

There are a few types of tenancy that *can't* be an Assured Short-hold Tenancy. These are:

- When the rent is more than £100,000 per year

- When the tenant is living in self-contained premises in the same building as the landlord (for example, a house has been converted into flats and you occupy the ground-floor flat while the tenant lives upstairs)

- When the property isn't the tenant's main home (they might have rented it just so they can stay there at week-ends, for example)

- When the tenant is a limited company

- When the property is a holiday let

- When the tenant is living with the landlord (as a lodger, for example)

In the case of holiday lets and lodgers, the tenant will occupy the property under license, meaning that they have no security of tenure and must leave when the agreement ends.

With a lodger, for example, you could verbally allow them to stay and then be within your rights to verbally ask them to leave a month later. You can (and should) still have a written agreement so you're both clear on what's expected, but this document wouldn't be an AST – it would be a license agreement.

The same goes for holiday lets: when someone stays in a hotel room, they actually occupy it under license, and holiday lets are no different. The occupant must leave when they're asked to (either verbally or in the contract), and if they felt you'd acted unfairly they'd have no particular law to fall back on – they'd have to take you to court for breach of contract.

In the other cases listed (such as if the tenant is a limited company), you will sign a *contractual tenancy agreement* with the tenant. This means that the Housing Act 1988 rights and responsibilities don't apply, so the landlord has more flexibility in the terms they set out. The tenant is still protected by the Unfair Terms in Consumer Contracts Regulations 1999, however, and the landlord still needs to abide by their repairing obligations in the Landlord and Tenant Act 1985.

In the rest of this chapter, I'll be talking specifically about ASTs because they cover the vast majority of situations. If you're planning to enter into an agreement that falls under one of the above categories, you should speak to a solicitor to get them to draw up an appropriate agreement.

Chapter 13

What should be in an AST?

As I mentioned earlier, a good tenancy agreement is a valuable document, because:

- It clearly sets out what's expected of both parties.

- It provides the correct legal footing to start, maintain and end the tenancy.

- It serves as a reference throughout the tenancy to see what should happen in certain situations.

To be truly useful, a tenancy agreement needs to be legally correct, easy to understand, and cover everything both parties need to know. In this chapter, we'll first look at the information you *should* include. After that, we'll move on to clauses that will apply whether you include them or not, and finally we'll look at things you *shouldn't* include.

The landlord's address

Section 48 of the Landlord and Tenant Act states that the tenant must be given an address in England or Wales where they can serve notices on the landlord – such as their notice to leave the property. This could be provided separately, but it's usually included in the tenancy agreement. If the tenant doesn't receive this information in one way or another, they don't legally have to pay rent – so, pretty important then.

The address doesn't have to be the landlord's residential address: it can be the address of the letting agent, a solicitor, a friend… anywhere that the message will actually be passed on. Many landlords prefer for the tenant not to know their home address, so at Yellow Lettings we include our own address on the tenancy agreement by default.

Another part of the Landlord and Tenant Act (Section 1), however, says that if the tenant specifically asks in writing for the landlord's actual address, they must receive a reply in writing within 21 days. It would be a criminal offence not to do so – and honestly, when your cellmate asks what you're in for, would you want to say something as uncool as "Well, I contravened Section 1 of the Landlord and Tenant Act"?

The occupants' details and property address

The tenancy agreement should include the full address of the property that is being let, and the full names of every person who's going to live there.

Some of the people living there will be *tenants*, but others might be *permitted occupiers*. Both should be listed separately on the tenancy agreement so it's clear which is which.

A tenant is someone who you'll put through the referencing process, and will be bound by the terms of the tenancy agreement. So if the rent is late, for example, you can pursue all tenants equally to make sure it's paid.

A permitted occupier is someone who has permission to live there, but doesn't contribute to the rent and isn't a party to the agreement. It's the responsibility of the tenants to make sure that their permitted occupiers stick to the terms of the tenancy agreement – and if the tenants leave for any reason, their permitted occupiers must go at the same time.

All children will be permitted occupiers, and normally all adults will be tenants. Sometimes, though, the occupants will want a particular adult *not* to be a tenant – such as an elderly relative. As a rule, it's legally the most straightforward if all adults are tenants – but this is one of those areas where there's no clear "right" answer and it very rarely crops up anyway. Take legal advice if it *does* crop up and you're at all concerned.

> *This is one of those occasions where having access to a free landlord helpline can be extremely handy. Register your copy of the book at www.propertygeek.net/landlord and I'll point you towards a landlord association that provides this service.*

As well as listing the names of every occupier, it's standard to include the following for each tenant:

- A phone number

- An email address

- Their current address

- A post-tenancy address where they can be reached (often a relative's address, because obviously they're unlikely to know where they'll be living next)

The term of the tenancy

Most tenancies are granted for an initial fixed term of 6 or 12 months, so the tenancy agreement should state the start and the end date.

A common area of misunderstanding is the assumption that if the tenancy reaches its end date without being renewed, the tenant must move out. This isn't true: by default, if no action is taken by either side, the tenancy continues on what's called a "statutory periodic" basis.

This means that the agreement continues as-is from period to period – with each period relating to the interval at which the rent is paid. If rent is paid monthly, the period is one month; if weekly, the period is one week; – and so on.

So at the end of the fixed term, there are three possibilities:

- The tenant can move out and the tenancy ends.

- The tenancy can continue as-is on a "statutory periodic" basis.

- The landlord and tenant can sign a new tenancy agreement (with the same terms or different ones) for another fixed period.

When we discuss the end of a tenancy in Section 5, we'll get into all this in a lot more detail. For now, you just have to know the following about the length of a tenancy term:

- A longer fixed term is *good* for you as a landlord because it means the tenant can't leave during it (unless there's a break clause), which delays the hassle and expense of the tenant moving out.

- But a longer fixed term is also *bad* because you can't end the tenancy and take back possession except in very particular circumstances.

- Don't feel that the length of the fixed term has to dictate exactly how long the tenant will actually live in your property: as mentioned, it can just continue on a periodic basis or be renewed if both sides are happy.

The length of the term will need to be negotiated with the tenant – including whether there'll be a "break clause", which is a point in the fixed term where either party can end the tenancy early. For example, you could sign a 12-month tenancy agreement, with a break clause after six months – meaning either party can serve notice to end the agreement after it's been running for six months. This break clause *must* be equally binding on both sides – that is, *either* party can execute the clause, and the period of notice required must be the same for both sides.

Letting agents in general are keen on keeping fixed terms short, because when a tenancy is renewed it gives them the opportunity to charge all kinds of imaginative fees to both tenant and landlord. As a landlord, you'll probably want to gravitate towards a longer fixed term for security – although you'll also want to weigh up the disadvantages of being in a fixed term if a tenant goes rogue (something we'll cover in Part 5).

In case you're wondering what we do at Yellow Lettings, we issue initial tenancy agreements for 12 months unless either party requests otherwise. Any longer is too much of a commitment (and the terms of most mortgages insist on a tenancy being granted for a maximum of 12 months), and any shorter doesn't provide the landlord with rental income for very long until we could potentially need to find another tenant again.

The amount of rent and how it's to be paid

When it comes to rent (the most important bit in your eyes, probably), the tenancy agreement should state:

- The amount of rent, and whether it's paid weekly or monthly (or any other period, but these are standard)

- That the rent should be paid in advance of each period

rather than in arrears – so for example, on 1st September the tenant needs to pay the rent that covers them up until 30th September

- That joint tenants are "jointly and severally liable" for the rent, meaning that if one tenant stops paying, the others will have to make up the difference – and they can all be pursued for any arrears, regardless of who is at fault

- The payment method that must be used (such as standing order, direct debit, cash or cheque)

- Whether the rent will increase during the fixed term, and how often it will be reviewed during the tenancy (more on this in Part 4)

The deposit

Treating the deposit correctly is *very* important, so a whole future chapter will be dedicated to it – including what needs to be said about the deposit in the tenancy agreement.

The notice needed to end the tenancy

As I'll explain in Part 5, there's a legal minimum amount of notice required by each party to end the tenancy: two months for the landlord, and one month for the tenant.

(This is a bit different if the rent is due less often than monthly – for example, quarterly – but this almost never happens in residential tenancies, so let's not worry about it.)

Even though this notice period is set in law and applies even if you say nothing about it in the tenancy agreement, you should still include it. Remember: the tenancy agreement is a "user manual" as well as a legal document, and your tenant is unlikely to be well versed in the finer points of the Housing Act 1988.

Useful optional clauses

The items listed above are the absolute bare minimum that must appear in a tenancy agreement, but a *good* agreement will include a lot more information: the one we use at Yellow Lettings runs to 11 pages.

Rather than running you point-by-point through an entire document, it's worth you spending a rip-roaring few minutes reading through the model tenancy agreement provided by the government to see the kind of information that's included. You can find it at www.propertygeek.net/modelagreement

Don't just use it (or any other agreement you find online or get sent by someone) as-is: remember, it's creating a legal agreement that gives your tenant important rights over an asset worth tens of thousands of pounds. Make sure your own agreement meets your needs, and – after you've written it – get it looked over by a solicitor if you're in any doubt.

I'll now run through some non-essential but useful clauses that we use at Yellow Lettings – which other landlords often include too. You can use some of these if you want or add your own: just bear in mind that when you're adding clauses of your own, they mustn't be "unfair" on the tenant. We'll see exactly what that means in practice shortly.

Service of documents by email

It will make your life substantially easier if you have the option of sending documents (such as those relating to the deposit) by email. But be aware that you'll need a clause expressly saying that the tenant consents to receiving communication by email – otherwise they could argue in court that the documents hadn't been validly served.

Even with this clause in place, you should still serve notice to end the tenancy by post – and we'll come back to this in more detail later.

Late rent

Rent is far more likely to be paid on time when there are consequences for it being late. As we'll see, a late rent clause can't be unfair ("The tenant will pay the landlord one trillion pounds if the rent isn't paid on the day it's due"), but you can charge a reasonable rate of interest on overdue rent as long as you say in the tenancy agreement that you will.

Prior notice of possession grounds

As we'll see later, there are two ways you can end a tenancy: the "no fault" Section 21 route, and the "here's my reason for wanting you gone" Section 8 route.

There are lots of reasons you're allowed to give when you go down the Section 8 route (known as "grounds"), and most of them relate to the tenant's behaviour. Other grounds, however, are more about your own situation – but you can only use them if you give advance notice in the tenancy agreement that you might rely on them later.

The most common is Ground 1: that you may require the property as your principal home after the end of the fixed term, or you previously occupied the property as your principal home. If you used to live at the property or you think there's any chance that you might want to live there yourself after the tenancy, this is worth chucking in – you'll find the wording in Annex 2 of the government's model agreement.

There are other more obscure grounds that require advance notice – such as that the property may be required for a minister of religion – but those aren't worth worrying about right now.

Pet clause

You don't have to let tenants keep pets. But if you're happy for them to do so, insert a clause with the pet's name, type of animal and breed, and say that no other animals may be kept without permission. This makes sure that they can't seek permission for a goldfish and open a small petting zoo in the living room.

Are you really going to insist that the tenant contacts you to amend the tenancy agreement when they find poor Jaws float-ing on the surface and rush out to the fair to win Nemo before the kids notice and get upset? No, you're not – but for more furry and bitey animals it's important to get specific about what you've agreed to.

Pests

You can't palm off all pest problems on tenants: if the pests were present at the start of the tenancy or the infestation is a result of a structural defect, it's your responsibility whatever the tenancy agreement says.

But it's handy to include a clause that says that in any other situation, pests are the tenant's responsibility to deal with. Pest control is expensive, and you don't want to bear the cost of removing critters that were attracted by a tenant's messy use of the property.

Garden maintenance

If the property has a garden, there should be a clause in the tenancy agreement stating who is responsible for maintaining it. Normally, you'll want this to be the tenant – and while includ-ing a clause doesn't mean they'll definitely be out there weeding the borders every weekend, it *does* mean that you can deduct gardening costs from their deposit if they don't keep on top of it.

You can't get overly prescriptive about the exact standard of upkeep, but a reasonable clause might call on the tenant to cut the grass as necessary, and keep other areas tidy, weed-free and in seasonal order. And of course, if you want it *back* in this condition, you must have *provided* it in this condition – backed up by a photographic inventory.

Tenants' contents insurance

Pro tip: "As a condition of our ASTs, tenants are required to have their own contents insurance. It means that if they have to move out (e.g. In the event of a fire or flood), they'll be covered for moving into emergency accommodation.

Also, if you're having unaccompanied tradespeople in your property, it's convenient for the tenant to blame them for stealing or breaking something. If the tradesperson denies it, we advise the tenant to make a police report and claim on their insurance. It prevents you from getting caught in the middle of a fictional or real problem." –Matt Elder

Rent review

We'll see more about increasing the rent in Part 4. For now, just know that it's helpful to have a "rent review" clause in place – something that says the rent will be reviewed annually and increased by a minimum percentage (such as RPI inflation).

You don't need to enforce this clause if you don't want to, but it's handy to have just in case.

Access for viewings

If you want to significantly cut down on gaps between tenants, you'll want to get access to carry out viewings while the existing tenants are still living there.

This is a pain for tenants so they won't always play ball, but your hand will be strengthened by adding a clause stating that tenants will give access for viewings at reasonable times upon receiving at least 24 hours' notice.

You're not realistically going to start ranting and raving about breach of contract if they refuse viewings, but it sets out your expectations and might make a difference if you gently remind them about the clause when they're not being overly helpful.

Informing third parties

There'll be lots of situations where it comes in handy to have a clause that allows you to contact and provide information to third parties.

A common one is dealing with utility bills that were left unpaid, where you might want to provide a forwarding address to the company. You might also want to provide the tenant's details to a tradesperson, so you don't have to pass messages back and forth when trying to arrange a safety check or a maintenance job.

This clause is also important when dealing with tenants on housing benefit, where you may need to correspond with the council about unpaid benefits that they owe you.

Payment of bills

It's worth having a clause explicitly stating that all bills are the tenant's responsibility and can never be transferred back to the landlord. This makes sure (for example) that if the tenant takes out a 12-month contract for broadband but leaves after six months, the remainder of the contract is definitely their responsibility.

It's also handy to say that payment of the TV licence is the tenant's responsibility in every circumstance, regardless of who the TV was provided by.

Chapter 14

Implied terms in tenancy agreements

As well as the terms that are expressly included in the tenancy agreement, each tenancy is also governed by *implied* terms – which apply whether they're written down or not, and can't be altered by anything that's written in the agreement itself.

A good tenancy agreement will take these implied terms and make them explicit, so everyone knows exactly where they stand – but even if there's no written document at all, these rights will still apply as they've been clearly established in housing law.

Quiet enjoyment

The tenant has the right to "quiet enjoyment", which means they can live peacefully in the property without interference from the landlord or anyone else. This means that you (or any agent or tradesperson working under your instructions) can't turn up at the front door unannounced, or let yourself in with a set of keys.

Yes: that means it's not strictly acceptable to just ring on the doorbell while you happen to be passing if you think of something you want to check. In practice, many tenants won't mind (or will just do a convincing job of pretending to be out if they want to avoid you), but if the relationship goes sour they could legitimately accuse you of violating their right to quiet enjoyment. They could even (under the Protection From Eviction Act 1977) take you to court for harassment.

The only exceptions are in the case of an emergency, such as fire or flood, where of course it's essential that action is taken immediately and the tenant may not be contactable.

Right of access

While you must allow the tenants quiet enjoyment, the Landlord and Tenant Act 1985 does give you (or somebody you nominate) the implied right to enter the property after giving at least 24 hours' written notice. "In writing" can be by text or email.

On receiving your written notice, the tenant can withhold permission if they want to – they don't need to give any particular reason. If they do this from time to time (maybe they want to be present when you visit but can't be available at that time), that's fine, and your right of access is balanced against their right to quiet enjoyment.

Where things get tricky is if the tenant continually refuses to give access, because it might mean you're unable to make repairs or meet obligations like conducting a gas safety check. In this situation it's a good idea to write to the tenant pointing out that:

- They will be liable for any deterioration to the property due to you being unable to carry out repairs.

- They can't bring a claim against you for any injury or damage they suffer related to the property, as you couldn't get access to repair the damage.

If the tenant still doesn't relent, you can apply to the court for an injunction to get entry. Rest assured, though, that it isn't common for things to get this far. As with all disputes, the key is to keep proof of letters sent and written records of everything you've done in case the matter goes to court – and to fight the temptation to just sod the law and turn up on the doorstep with your scariest-looking mate…

"Tenant-like" occupation

The tenant has the implied obligation to occupy the property in a "tenant-like manner", which basically means taking care of the property as if it were their own home. This boils down to keeping on top of small day-to-day maintenance tasks themselves, such as:

- Changing lightbulbs

- Changing batteries in smoke detectors

- Unblocking toilets and sinks

- Mowing lawns and keeping the garden tidy (unless stated otherwise in the tenancy agreement)

- Repairing any damage that they or their guests accidentally cause (except for "fair wear and tear", which we'll see more of later)

The landlord shouldn't be bothered by having to deal with "everyday" matters like these, and would have a good case for recharging the tenant for any costs incurred relating to these issues – like a tradesperson's visit to unblock a sink on the tenant's behalf. They could also claim against the tenant for any damage that resulted from the property not being occupied in a "tenant-like manner" – like a blocked sink causing a flood, which damages the bathroom floor.

As I said at the start of this section, it's a good idea to make these implied terms explicit in the tenancy agreement. To avoid confrontation later, you can include a short list of the typical jobs that are the tenant's responsibility – so when you give them short shrift on the phone after they've asked you to change their lightbulb, you'll have a document to back you up.

Repairs

Regardless of what it says in the tenancy agreement (including if the agreement says nothing), you as the landlord have certain implied obligations when it comes to making repairs to the property.

Under the Landlord and Tenant Act 1985, you're obliged to keep the following in a good state of repair:

- The structure and exterior of the building (including drains, gutters and external pipes)

- Installations for the supply of water, gas, electricity and sanitation (including basins, sinks and baths)

- Installations for heating and hot water

The obligations don't extend to repairing anything that has ceased to function as a result of a tenant's negligence or failure to occupy the property in a "tenant-like manner".

Once you're aware of the need for a repair to one of these items, you're required to make the repair in a "reasonable" period of time. If you fail to do so, the tenant is entitled to withhold rent – even if you've written into the tenancy agreement that they can't – meaning they should set it aside and only pay it over to you once the repair has been made.

In addition to these obligations, you also need to make sure that the property is fit for occupation under the the page-turner that is the Housing Health and Safety Rating System (HHSRS), which lists 29 hazards relating to damp, mould, security, accidents and more. If the local authority inspects the property and finds it to be hazardous, they may take enforcement action – which might involve issuing you a notice that requires you to improve the property, or even remedying the hazard themselves and charging you for it.

Failing to stay on top of repairs can also make it more difficult to end the tenancy; more on this in Part 5.

Chapter 15

Unfair terms in tenancy agreements

You can add anything you like to a tenancy agreement. Sometimes – like we've seen in the case of when a tenant has a pet – it's useful to do so, because it clarifies how the landlord/tenant relationship will operate and what's expected of each party.

But that doesn't mean you can expect to be backed up by a judge when the tenant refuses to clean the windows at 3pm on the dot every Sunday – because "unfair terms" in contracts are unenforceable. While they don't invalidate the whole contract, they can't be relied on in court and may result in action by the Office of Fair Trading.

"Unfair terms" are those that remove a legal right that the tenant should have, or otherwise tip the balance of rights and responsibilities unfairly against the tenant.

"Removing a legal right" covers anything in the implied terms, and more. For example, you can't add a clause saying "The tenant will be responsible for sanitation, heating, and all repairs to the structure of the building", because these are the legal responsibility of the landlord. Similarly, you can't have a term saying "The landlord can pop around whenever she feels like it to help herself to biscuits", because that goes against the right to quiet enjoyment.

There are also many types of clause that would be unfair by tipping the balance against the tenant. These include imposing unreasonable charges (such as "The tenant will pay a fee of £1,000 for any missed appointment") or unreasonable obligations (like "The tenant must send photos every evening to show that the house is tidy"). It sounds daft, but a solicitor did tell me about one tenancy agreement where the landlord had specified that the hedge outside must be trimmed into the shape of a peacock at all times…

Chapter 16

Moving the tenants in

With the tenancy agreement drawn up, it's *so nearly* time to bank the first month's rent and catch up on the Bake-Off episodes you've missed while sorting all this out – but not before you've made some final preparations and conducted an inventory…

Final preparations

In the run-up to the tenants moving in, it's good practice to give them a draft copy of the tenancy agreement to read through – ideally seven days ahead of move-in, if time allows. This will give them time to query anything they're unclear on or aren't happy with, so they can't claim later that you ambushed them with the agreement on move-in day and they weren't able to read it properly.

While they're doing that, you can be running around making sure the property is spick and span. If it's just been refurbished, make sure all the jobs have been completed and there are no materials left lying around in cupboards. If tenants have moved out, check that all their things have gone and you've sorted any defects that were listed on the check-out report. If you're moving out so that tenants can move in, do a slow and thorough walkthrough to make sure everything is in order: after years of living there, you could easily be immune to the loose handle on the kitchen drawer or not even notice the boxes stored on top of the wardrobe.

In any of those scenarios, check that all the basics are working: heating, hot water, no leaks, no dripping taps, doors and windows locking properly and opening without being stiff, and so on. If you don't check them now, you'll only have the tenant calling you to point them out when they notice – and you'll have to fix them at a potentially less convenient time. It's extremely common, for example, for a change of tenancy to happen in June only for a broken boiler to be noticed when it starts getting chilly in September. (Which, of course, is when gas engineers are at their busiest too.)

I'd also recommend getting the property professionally cleaned before letting it for the first time. Even if you've just finished fully refurbishing, there will be dust on surfaces (and inside cupboards) and possibly dirty footprints to deal with.

The advantage of a professional clean is that the tenancy agreement will state that the property must be given back in the same state as it was received – and if that state was "almost blinded by all the gleaming", there's less leeway for differences of opinion about whether it's *still* in that state at the end. You can't insist that an outgoing tenant pays for a professional clean (this would be considered an unfair term), but you *can* insist that it's cleaned "to a professional standard" – as long as the property met that standard when they moved in in the first place.

Drawing up an inventory

In this book we've already seen some good reasons for having a thorough inventory – such as to be clear about who's responsible for the safety of particular electrical items and whose contents are covered in the event of an insurance claim.

But here's the most important reason: without an inventory, you'll have a hard time making any deductions from your tenant's deposit when they move out, because you won't have a record of the state the property was in at the start.

There's really no reason *not* to have a good inventory, yet the majority of problems that landlords have in making damage claims result from not having their paperwork in order.

A good inventory will specify in detail what each item in a property is and what condition it's in – all the way down to "brass dimmer switch – as new" and "skirting boards painted with gloss white paint – good and clean". It should also have photographs (including close-ups of any damage), and some inventories even include a video.

You can conduct an inventory yourself, but I'd recommend using a professional: it's been known for landlords to lose deposit claims because they did their own inventory and therefore can't be considered to be neutral and objective. A professional will also be able to use the correct language (including a whole array of vocabulary for things like curtain poles that you'd never know existed) to clearly describe each item. The cost for a professional inventory depends on the size of the property, but you're probably looking at anything from £60 to £250.

The inventory should be conducted *before* the tenant moves any of their possessions in, and a copy given to them at check-in. They should be asked to initial each page and return a copy within a certain period of time to show that they agree, to prevent any disputes later. (If they don't return it, the tenancy agreement can state that this is taken as them agreeing.)

Checking the tenants in

The check-in should be conducted in person at the property itself, and is vital in making sure the documentation is correct and the tenant is ready to settle nicely into their new home.

Before the check-in takes place, you'll need to have received the first month's rent and the deposit in cleared funds – meaning if they paid by cheque, the funds have actually been paid into your bank account so you know it hasn't bounced.

Documentation

At check-in, you'll be presenting your tenants with a big old pile of documents:

- The tenancy agreement

  (The tenants should have received a draft copy in

advance, to give them time to read it and query anything without any time pressure. At check-in it *must* be signed by all tenants *and* any guarantors before the keys are handed over.)

- A copy of that old favourite, the EPC

- A copy of the gas safety certificate

- A copy of the government's (somewhat pointless) "How to rent" leaflet, if the property is in England (it's not needed in Wales)

  (Download the latest version by searching gov.uk for "How to rent".)

- A copy of the prescribed information and terms and conditions relating to the scheme you're using to protect the tenants' deposit (of which more in the next chapter)

- A copy of the inventory for them to sign and return later

- A standing order form – if that's how the rent will be paid

  (Ideally they'll fill it out there and then; you can post it back to their bank to make sure it doesn't get forgotten.)

- A photograph or photocopy of the keys (and any fobs for communal doors) that you're handing over, so you have a record of how many keys they've been given and therefore how many you need to get back at the end

All of these documents must be signed for, so if necessary you can prove in court that you've provided everything you were supposed to. You might want to create one sheet of paper listing everything you've provided, and just get a signature at the bottom of that (although the tenancy agreement, inventory and standing order form should be signed separately too).

If you prefer, you can save a small spinney worth of trees and provide all these documents digitally – which is what we do at Yellow Lettings. Using a digital signing service like Echosign (www.echosign.com), Hellosign (www.hellosign.com) or Signable (www.signable.co.uk) establishes a legally binding audit trail, and automatically emails a copy to the tenant so they have it for future reference.

Meter readings

At the check-in, you should also take meter readings – which you'll need when you inform the utility suppliers about the change of occupancy (something we'll come back to in a future chapter). Also note down the meter serial numbers if you don't have them already.

House manual

There's no legal requirement (in England and Wales) to provide any kind of information pack about the property itself, but I recommend doing so. If nothing else, it will save you from fielding phone calls with questions down the line. It's also a good opportunity to provide any safety information.

It's worth including information like:

- The location of the stopcock

- How to set and disarm the alarm (if there is one)

- The National Gas Emergency Service number (0800 111 999) to call in the event of smelling gas

- The number to call in case of a power cut (the number is 105 – a service that will connect you to the local network operator)

- Your contact details, when you're willing to be contacted, and who to call in the case of an emergency outside these hours

- Instructions for using the boiler and central heating

- A reminder of the requirement for them to regularly test the smoke alarms

- Descriptions of how to use any other features of the property that aren't entirely straightforward

- Any maintenance tasks that you recommend carrying out to avoid issues (like regularly removing hair from the plughole to avoid a blockage)

- Information about local council services, like when the

bins are collected and who to call to remove bulky rubbish

- Information about any local highlights that they might enjoy, like restaurants and cultural activities

Pro tip: "Heating and hot water tend to cause issues for new tenants getting used to the system – and they can think there's a fault when it's actually just the settings. Put together a decent set of instructions, including photos, to tell the tenants how everything works and where the controls and switches are located – which in the case of one of my properties are hidden in the wardrobes!" –David Barker

Will tenants read and remember all of this? Realistically, no – but anything they *do* retain will save a phone call, and it also shows that you're a professional landlord who cares about them understanding and enjoying their new home.

Appliance manuals

It might seem daft on the face of it, but it's an important safety requirement to provide manuals for any electrical appliances that form part of the inventory. You might argue that it's pretty bloomin' obvious how a fridge works, but if the tenant causes a fire by plugging it into a four-way adapter with their hairdryer and straighteners, it could be argued in court that the tenant didn't have proper guidance about how to use it safely.

Check-in is a good time to make sure the manuals are present and correct – and that the tenant knows where to find them. If the appliances are old and the manuals have been lost, you can usually download and re-print manuals from the manufacturers' websites.

Chapter 17

Protecting the deposit

Before the current deposit protection system came into effect in 2007, the landlord held all the cards with regard to whether a tenant would get their deposit back. They could decide on whatever deductions they wanted, and the tenant would have very little power to challenge it – so they'd often just write off the idea of ever seeing their deposit again.

Under the new system, the landlord must register the deposit with one of three government-approved schemes. At the end of the tenancy, if there's a dispute about the deductions that should be made (due to damage or unpaid bills), the scheme will mediate the situation. From a landlord's side this isn't perfect – it's more paperwork, and the perception is that the tenant is favoured when there's a dispute – but it's hard to argue that it's not fairer.

Even though deposit protection has been in place for ten years, plenty of landlords still haven't got the memo about how deposits should be handled – and to be fair to them, there are non-obvious aspects to the rules you need to follow. Nevertheless, the penalties for getting it wrong can be severe, so in this chapter I'll tell you exactly what to do when you receive a tenant's deposit – after first scaring you a little about what could happen if you don't…

The price of getting it wrong...

Incorrectly handling a tenant's deposit is probably the most common mistake that amateur landlords make – and if they're unlucky, the lesson can be a *very* expensive one.

There are two aspects to handling a deposit correctly:

1. You must register it with a government-approved scheme. (Most landlords now know that they're obligated to do this.)

2. You must issue (and in some cases re-issue at the appropriate time) the tenant with certain legally required information about the deposit. (Many landlords are totally unaware of the need to do this.)

The penalty for getting it wrong is also twofold:

1. A court can issue you with a fine of up to three times the amount of the deposit in question.

2. Until the matter has been rectified, you can't use the most straightforward way of ending the tenancy (a Section 21 notice) and getting the property back. (I'll go into lots more detail about the Section 21 notice in Part 5.)

As it happens, tenants are also largely clueless about the law regarding how their deposit should be treated, so on most occasions a landlord will never be challenged if they get it wrong. There are rumours, however, that deposit protection is going to be the next "PPI": companies will crop up and speculatively approach tenants to see if their deposit was mishandled, and take a cut of any compensation paid. If this happens, landlords are far less likely to get away with even an honest mistake.

Suitably terrified? OK, then let's make sure you get it right.

Registering the deposit

Since April 2007, it's been mandatory to register new deposits with a tenancy deposit protection (TDP) service. There are three to choose from:

- mydeposits – www.mydeposits.co.uk

- Deposit Protection Service (DPS) – www.depositprotec-tion.com

- Tenancy Deposit Scheme (TDS) – www.tenancydeposits-cheme.com

All three of the services offer an *insurance-backed* scheme, which means that you don't have to physically pay the deposit over to them – you just make them aware of the deposit's existence and keep it in your own bank account for the duration of the tenancy. The DPS and mydeposits also offer a *custodial* scheme, where you actually transfer the deposit into their bank account.

Some landlords prefer the insurance-backed route because they don't have to physically transfer the money across and wait for it to come back. Personally, I prefer the custodial route so I know the money in my account is all actually "mine".

Another factor is that the custodial schemes are free (presumably because they make money on the interest the deposits collect while in their bank accounts), whereas the insurance-backed schemes have a charge of around £15 to £30.

There's not a lot of difference between the three companies themselves: at Yellow Lettings we use the custodial scheme from the DPS, but don't have any strong feelings about it. Whichever service you choose, you can follow the steps on their website to register the deposit online in a relatively straightforward manner.

Issuing the "prescribed information"

Here's where landlords screw up: they think that simply registering the deposit is enough. It isn't: you *also* need to issue your tenants with "prescribed information", which tells them who is holding the deposit, the monetary amount of the deposit, what to do in the event of a dispute, and several other pieces of information.

This prescribed information can either form part of the tenancy agreement or be issued separately – it doesn't matter which, but it *must* be separately signed by the landlord and tenant if it doesn't form part of the tenancy agreement.

And there's more! Protecting the deposit and issuing what *appears* to be the full prescribed information isn't enough, because you *also* need to issue them with a copy of the scheme's "information for tenants" or "terms and conditions" leaflet (depending on the service), which can run to 20+ pages of nonsense that nobody is ever going to read.

And no, you can't just provide them with a link to where the T&Cs can be read online: you need to print it all out, or include it in full in the documents you're delivering digitally.

So in summary, correctly protecting a deposit means that you've:

- Registered the deposit with one of the three services

- Given the tenant the prescribed information (either as part of the tenancy agreement or separately) and had them sign it

- Also given them the service's leaflet for tenants with the full terms and conditions

The time limit

Can you just do this whenever you next wake up on a Sunday feeling like having a bit of an admin day? Nope – all of this (protecting the deposit and serving the required information) must be accomplished within 30 days of receiving the deposit.

Note: that's within 30 days of *receiving the deposit* – **not** within 30 days of the tenancy starting. Also, if you receive the deposit in the form of a cheque, the clock starts on the day that the cheque physically comes into your possession – not when the funds clear into your account.

This is up from 14 days when the schemes first came into existence, so think yourself lucky.

Chapter 18

Telling the utility suppliers and council

With the tenants in and the deposit protected, you can *nearly* breathe a sigh of relief and wait for the next month's rental payment to hit your bank account... but not quite. First, you need to make a few organisations aware of the change of occupancy.

Utility suppliers

I'm pretty sure you've got enough bills of your own without getting stuck with someone else's, so it's important to let the utility suppliers know the details of the new tenants. This is why you took the meter readings at check-in – because the suppliers will need to know:

- The final meter readings

- The new address of the previous occupier. If the first set of tenants has just moved in, this is you. If you had tenants previously, their forwarding address should be included on their old tenancy agreement

- The names of the new tenants

They will then send a final bill to the previous occupier (or you), and a letter to the new occupier inviting them to set up their account.

By the way, tenants in general are free to change their utility suppliers as they see fit – but it's worth stating in the tenancy agreement (and making clear in the house manual, which they're more likely to read) that they should let you know who the new suppliers are.

Council tax department

You definitely don't want to get stuck with a council tax bill, so it's essential to provide the council with details of the new occupiers and let them know the date they moved in. Most local councils have an online form you can use.

Everyone else

If the property used to be your home and you're moving out to let it to tenants, you're going to have to make *all* kinds of companies aware that you've moved. It's important to do so, because it's not your tenants' responsibility to forward on your general mail – and nor should they have you popping over every week to pick it up.

If you'll still be living within the UK, you could set up forwarding with the Royal Mail for a few months, which means that any post addressed to you will get forwarded on to the address you specify. Then, as each letter arrives with a "redirection" sticker on it, you can add that sender to your list of companies to contact and blast through them all on a (really, really boring) weekend morning. Then go out for cake.

Conclusion to Part 3

High-fives all round! The contract is signed, the deposit is protected, and the tenants are deciding whether the pot plant looks better by the window or next to the sofa. You're done!

Now would be a good time to breathe a sigh of relief and / or pat yourself on the back – it's no mean feat to have reached this stage and done everything correctly.

> *I've put together a checklist of all the major steps involved in getting to this point, which I'll send you when you register your copy of this book at www.propertygeek.net/landlord – so you won't run the risk of forgetting something vital!*

But without wanting to be Mr Misery over here, in a way your work is just getting started – because now you've got a customer, and keeping them happy and everything running smoothly isn't exactly a walk in the park either. Managing the property effectively is the key to having tenants who are happy, pay up, stay for a long time and take good care of your investment – so the next section is all about how to do exactly that…

PART 4:
MANAGING THE TENANCY

Introduction

Property: sparkling and ready!

Tenants: found!

Tenancy: all set up, check-in done and deposit protected!

So… now what?

Well, that depends on how things go. If you're lucky, there'll just be a few regular jobs to take care of: routine inspections, the odd bit of normal maintenance, and renewing the tenancy when your happy tenants want to stay longer.

If you're *not* so lucky, there could also be emergency repairs to arrange and non-payment of rent to resolve.

In Part 4 we'll run through all these situations and more – starting with some general advice about how to interact with your happy new tenants.

Chapter 19

Communicating with your tenants

Now that your tenants have moved in, the next thing you need to do is... well, who knows? Shortly we'll run through all the actions you *might* need to take, but first it's worth considering some general principles for keeping a tenancy running smoothly.

The first thing to remember is that *your property is now their home*, and you now know that "quiet enjoyment" means you can only access the property with their permission after giving appropriate notice. It sounds insultingly obvious to point that out, but you'd be surprised by how many landlords don't fully appreciate this point. Especially if they've previously lived in the property, they think it's OK to let themselves in to pick up the post or ring on the doorbell while passing to check on how a repair is holding up.

The next thing to consider is general ground rules for communication. I recommend encouraging text-based communication wherever possible: email worked well for me when I was self-managing, but texting or a messaging service like WhatsApp is fine too.

> *Pro tip: "We use a WhatsApp group per property, with all ten-ants and landlords as members. Texts feel less formal and easier to send, and so tenants communicate better. We also thank tenants for telling us about problems." –Elizabeth and Vientiene Ta'eed*

Text-based communication is beneficial for two reasons. Firstly, it's generally more convenient: you don't have to stop what you're doing to answer the phone, and they can send messages whenever they think of it rather than wait for a suitable time to call. The second benefit is that it provides a written record: if you get into a dispute and they claim that you've left a repair ignored for weeks on end, you can easily retort by showing your time-stamped replies where you offered to fix it.

If I were you, I wouldn't give out your personal mobile number – just in case your lovely-on-day-one tenant turns out not to be as friendly or amenable as you first thought. Instead, you could get a cheap second phone with a prepaid SIM, or a Skype num-ber that forwards to your main phone. Alternatively, you could sign up with a service like Switchboard Free (www.switch-boardfree.com), which can forward calls and take messages.

I also recommend being disciplined about only replying to non-emergency messages within normal working hours. You might not mind replying to a 10pm text straight away *this* time, but it sets an expectation. Being responsive and helpful is important, but there's no law that says renting out a property means you need to provide a 24/7 helpline (although the way the government is going, it's only a matter of time).

> *Pro tip: "Use a simple CRM (Customer Relationship Management) system to store tenants' contact details and make notes on any conversation you had with them. If you ever get into a 'he said, she said' situation and you've made notes, it will be easy to get to the bottom of things. A system like Less Annoying CRM (www.lessannoyingcrm.com) is relatively cheap." –Matt Elder*

With ground rules set, the final thing to do is make a note of key dates in the lifecycle of the tenancy – such as:

- A recurring reminder for the monthly rent due date, so you can check that it's been paid

- The expiry date of the annual gas safety certificate (if you have a gas supply)

- The end date of the fixed-term tenancy

- The date two months before the end of the fixed-term tenancy (for reasons that will become clear in Part 5)

- Dates of any inspections you plan to make

You can use whatever system works for you, but I organise my life with Google Calendar (calendar.google.com). The handy thing about this and similar online services is you can put in a date and also ask to get an alert a set amount of time *before* that date. For example, you can diarise the date that your gas safety certificate expires and also get an alert one month beforehand, so you've got ample time before expiry to book in the inspection.

> *Pro tip: "I have a Google Drive folder set up as a go-to place for all my property files: inventories, tenancy agreements, deposit protection information, EPCs, etc. I have a folder for each property, and separate folders for all my finance information, receipts, spreadsheets, etc. My whole property business is safely stored away, but accessible from anywhere!" –Tory Ion-Webb*

Chapter 20

How to deal with non-payment of rent

OK, that's the niceties out of the way. Now let's dive head-on into every landlord's biggest fear: not getting paid.

Whatever the reason, not getting paid is *bad*. The obvious reason is that you'll need to cover your mortgage and other expenses without any cash coming in. But you also need to remember that the longer you go without being paid, the more likely it is that you'll *never* get paid.

How best to deal with it? Like a ninja attack: quickly, effectively, and while wearing a black bandana. OK, maybe not that last one.

How the rent should be paid

Rent is most commonly paid by standing order. If you followed the steps in the last section when it came to setting up the tenancy, you'll have asked the tenant to fill in a standing order form – and then you'll have posted it to their bank yourself to make sure there's no way they forget to do it.

Another option is direct debit, which comes with some significant advantages. At Yellow Lettings we use a service called GoCardless (www.gocardless.com) to manage direct debits. It's helpful for many reasons:

- You just send the tenant a link and they can complete the process of setting up the direct debit online. Dead easy for them (so they're more likely to do it), and you'll be notified when it's been set up successfully.

- You'll be alerted if a scheduled payment is missed.

- You'll be alerted if the arrangement is cancelled by the tenant.

The downside? It isn't free – although it's really not extortionate either. The GoCardless fee is capped at £2 per transaction.

However the rent is to be received, schedule the rent due date in your calendar and check your bank account on that day to see if it's come in.

> Pro tip: "I send a receipt for the rent each month, and on the bottom I include a few key pieces of information – like what to do if they smell gas, a reminder to check smoke alarms regularly, and my phone number." –Justyn Evans

If the first rent payment is late...

... it means one of two things: either there's been a cock-up with setting up the standing order or direct debit (no real biggie), or the tenant is already unable or unwilling to pay (a very big biggie indeed).

It's vital that you get onto it right away, to send the message that the "rent due date" isn't a guideline or an aspiration: *it's the date on which the rent will be paid*. For a minority of tenants, bizarrely, paying for the roof over their head seems to be the bottom of their list of priorities – and every other bill, vice and whim will be the focus of their cash if you're not firm from the start.

Depending on your style, I'd recommend contacting the tenant on the evening of the day the rent was due to question what's happened to it: you don't have to be accusatory (and nor should you be, because it could be an innocent mistake), but just making contact on the day itself makes the point that this is something you take very seriously.

Chances are that it's just something innocent – like the standing order not being set up correctly. But still, be on the lookout for excuses. Most tenants are perfectly upstanding individuals, but the bad ones can do an excellent impression of being an upstanding individual and string you along for weeks with perfectly plausible excuses and apologies.

> *Pro tip: "I make it clear from the start that the rent due date is the day the money should be in my account – not the day for a debit to*

be taken from their account. The result is that, in the majority of cases, the rent is usually in my account early!" –Carol Duckfield

If a subsequent rent payment is late...

… again, get on it right away: this time you know that the arrangement was set up correctly in the first place, so it's even more of a red flag if it suddenly doesn't turn up. Has the tenant cancelled the arrangement, or has it failed because there isn't enough money in their account?

And again, be very wary of excuses and sob stories. Tenants do sometimes genuinely fall on hard times, but if it's a genuine shortfall then they should show willing by offering you part-payment and committing to when you'll get the rest. The important thing is to push for an honest dialogue – which isn't easy, because good people who've fallen on tough times can be too embarrassed to admit that they can't pay you.

If you've taken out Rent Guarantee Insurance (discussed back in Part 1), make sure you check the terms of your agreement: it's often a requirement that you make the insurer aware of a missed payment within a certain timeframe. (This advice applies if it's the very first missed payment too.)

If the situation isn't resolved quickly...

If it's not an honest mistake – or a one-off shortfall where the tenant is straightforward with you and commits to a firm plan to put things right – you don't want to let things drag on for any longer than they have to. As I said at the start of this chapter, the longer things go on, the less likely you are ever to get paid. Once someone's behind with their bills in general, how likely to do you think they are four months later to suddenly get everything back on track and send you the lump of arrears they've built up?

Unfortunately, whether you're the victim of a "can't pay" or "won't pay" situation, the result is the same: legal action. It's expensive, time-consuming, hard to get right and all-in-all no fun for anyone. We'll be coming back to this sorry point in Part 5.

Don't panic!

I'm not trying to scare you with all this talk about not getting paid, and it's important to remember that genuine horror stories are rare. I've never had one, for example (he says, touching every bit of wood in sight), but it's really no fun at all when it *does* happen. Even writing this chapter has proven difficult when it comes to getting the balance of language right. On the one hand, you're dealing with people – and unpredictable, inexplicable and unfortunate things can happen whenever human beings are involved. But on the other hand, it's dangerous to give the benefit of the doubt, because rogue tenants often seem entirely plausible.

At Yellow, we've inherited some tenancies to which we can't apply our normal rent guarantee, and these take up a disproportionate amount of our time. In almost every case it's not malicious – these are tenants who are struggling but doing their best, or who make an honest mistake – but it's still draining and immensely time-consuming to sort out. If you're doing it on your own, without much experience and working around a full-time job, it's even more of a challenge.

That's why prevention is so much better than needing to come up with a cure when it comes to rent arrears. There are two main types of prevention:

- Choose the right tenant in the first place. You can never be 100% sure, but comprehensive referencing plus gut feel will get you a very long way.

- Jump straight onto any payment issues the second they arise, and don't take any nonsense: if you send the right message at the start, you're less likely to have problems down the line.

OK, that's quite enough about non-payment of rent. Let's move on to happier matters: emergencies! Oh.

Chapter 21

Dealing with emergencies

I'm really front-loading this section with the bad stuff, huh?

Managing a property involves two different types of responsibility: proactively taking care of routine maintenance and safety issues, and reacting to any emergencies that arise.

What is an emergency? Basically, it's anything that will have an impact on the health, safety or wellbeing of your tenants, or cause damage to the property, if it's not dealt with pronto. A non-exhaustive list would include:

- The heating not working

- A plumbing fault rendering the only toilet or washing facilities unusable

- Damage to windows or doors that puts the tenants at risk of someone breaking in

- A burst pipe causing flooding

- An electrical failure

You'll notice that this is very similar to the list of your statutory responsibilities that we went over in Part 3 – which makes sense, because it's obviously worth making you legally responsible for taking care of these essential issues.

Agreeing on a definition of "emergency"

While the list above is non-exhaustive, a full list still wouldn't include items like "There's an unsightly mark on the coffee table and the vicar is coming around for tea tomorrow" or "A handle has come off a cupboard and now I'm at risk of breaking a nail by opening it from the side." But people are weird, so it's worth defining in your house manual what qualifies as an emergency and what, quite frankly, doesn't.

All the time I hear people say things like: "I could never be a landlord – I couldn't deal with a tenant calling me up at 3am complaining that a lightbulb's gone" – which is frankly ridiculous, because (a) you could just use a managing agent if you weren't so tight, and (b) if you pick the right tenant, set expectations and communicate effectively, you'll never have a tenant contacting you out of hours about something non-urgent.

It's true, though, that there's often a blurry line between "true emergency" and "very annoying and needs to be sorted quickly, but not actually an emergency". For example, it's very common for problems to be reported after 5pm – which is when tenants tend to be around to notice them, but also when it's very difficult to get a tradesperson out at a reasonable price.

If I discovered at 7pm that the heating in my own home wasn't working, I'd put on an extra jumper and wait until the next day to get someone out – and unless there are special circumstances, I'd expect tenants to do the same. The key in this situation is good communication: if the tenant realises that you're taking it seriously and it will be sorted as soon as reasonably possible, they're less likely to kick up a fuss about it not being done *now*.

But what about *real* emergencies – where life and limb are threatened if action isn't taken immediately?

The return of the house manual

For most emergencies, the most appropriate action probably won't be for the tenant to attempt to rouse you from your bed at 3am. While there may or may not be something you can do about it, it's still not a sensible plan because the tenant won't be able to guarantee getting hold of you instantly.

So it's a good idea to cover in the house manual what to do in the main categories of emergency situation:

- If the house is on fire, they should call 999 (duh).

- If they smell gas, provide the National Gas Emergency Service number (0800 111 999) and tell them to turn off the supply at the meter.

- If the electricity goes off, say where the consumer unit

(fuse box) is to check the fuses, and tell them to just flick the switch back if one of them is in the wrong position. Also provide the electrical company's number to check if it's a broader outage.

- If there's a leak, say where the stopcock is (and how to use it) so they can turn off the water until they can get hold of you (or your appointed person) to investigate.

- If they lock themselves out, provide the number of a local 24/7 locksmith – and make them aware that they will need to pay *and* immediately give you a copy of the new key.

It's rare that an emergency *can't* wait until the next day if the action above is taken. And if you make clear that they can't rely on reaching you immediately at any time, the tenants should be prepared to take appropriate measures themselves in the first instance.

If you're willing to pay a tiny monthly fee, however, there's an even better solution to dealing with emergencies…

Landlord emergency cover

Something I've started doing with all my properties is buying a policy called "landlord emergency cover" – which, as the name suggests, covers you in the event of emergency up to a certain limit.

The best thing (in my view) about emergency cover is that the insurance company provides you with a 24-hour hotline – and if you pass this to your tenants along with your policy number (which can go in the house manual), the tenant can call them directly and sort it out without you needing to be involved at all!

Policies vary, but the one I use covers me for repairs up to £500 for anything to do with:

- Heating failure

- Electrical failure

- Plumbing failure and leaks

- The security of doors and windows

- Vermin

So if something goes wrong, the tenant can call the insurer – who'll sort everything out for me. If the cost (of the callout plus any subsequent work to rectify the problem) is under £500, I don't have to pay anything.

> *There are plenty of options out there, but I'll send you the details of the company I currently use when you register your copy of this book at www.propertygeek.net/landlord*

You can also take out policies that specifically cover just your boiler – such as HomeCare from British Gas.

Chapter 22

Arranging (non-emergency) repairs

However top-notch your property and gentle your tenant, repairs will be required at some point. Either you'll notice something in a routine inspection that clearly needs attention soon, or you'll get a call that something has suddenly broken – but either way, you'll have to get on the case and sort it out.

My golden rule of repairs is: *if something needs fixing or replacing, do it NOW.*

Let me clarify, because I'm by no means suggesting that you get someone out within the hour on Christmas Day, then pay them a ludicrous call-out fee while they moan about all the mince pies they're missing. I just mean: don't dilly-dally in the hopes that the tenant will forget about it, or it will miraculously go away, or you'll get a big Premium Bond win to ease your cashflow situation.

By waiting, you're only going to accomplish two things:

- You'll annoy the tenant (who is the customer after all), who might then start looking elsewhere if they feel like they're not getting value for money or that their needs aren't being met.

- You run the risk of the issue getting worse, and therefore being even more expensive to fix by the time you get around to it.

This is why it's imperative that you build an allowance for repairs into your figures, and always have cash on hand to deal with anything that comes up. A common figure to put aside is 10% of the rent – or you might just decide to keep a "float" of a couple of thousand pounds, which you top up every time you need to dip into it.

When is maintenance your responsibility?

Just because something's broken, it doesn't mean it's necessarily your responsibility to fix it. Remember the phrase from the tenancy agreement about occupying the property in a "tenant-like manner"? This basically means that the tenant should be expected to take care of routine odd jobs, and not expect you to be their mother or servant when the tiniest thing needs doing. Changing a lightbulb or unblocking a sink would clearly fall into this category.

Then there are jobs that are clearly your responsibility. That's anything included in those "implied terms" that you're liable for even if the tenancy agreement is silent about them: the structure of the building, heating and hot water, sanitation, and so on.

If something falls into the second category, you're duty-bound to deal with it in a "reasonable" amount of time. If it falls into the first category, you might decide to do it anyway to keep the peace, but there's a risk that they'll make a habit of turning to you whenever the slightest thing needs doing. I recommend that you politely point out that it's not your responsibility, and give some pointers about what they should do: if someone is renting for the first time, they can't necessarily be expected to know where the line is supposed to be drawn.

Finding a tradesperson

When repairs *are* your responsibility, you can, of course, do them yourself. But please: only do this if you know you can do the work to a professional standard, and you hold any certificates necessary to do certain types of work. I absolutely *can't* do work to any standard other than "childlike and reckless", so I'm well-versed in the art of finding tradespeople.

In time, you'll build up a little black book of reliable trades to cover all the major areas – general maintenance, plumbing, decorating, electrical work, etc. – but at first, you'll probably need to be in "reactive" mode and go searching for someone every time an issue comes up.

Pro tip: "Good tradespeople have a shelf-life: over time, expect someone who has provided a good service to start letting you down. Someone who's good tends to find that their volume of work grows through repeat business and referrals, but the size of their business doesn't – so you won't be able to get hold of them for weeks, or their quality of work will suffer. You just have to accept this and try to have multiple tradespeople on hand for each type of job you may encounter – which is easier said than done." – Matt Elder

As I mentioned way back at the start (when we were talking about getting your property ready to let in the first place), I'm a big fan of sites like MyBuilder (www.mybuilder.com): it saves ringing round because you just post your job, have tradespeople approach you, and look at their reviews to get a feel for whether they're any good. Unless I have a personal recommendation (which is always the best way, and a big benefit of getting to know other landlords in your local area), this is my go-to method.

Pro tip: "Look for reviews of the specific type of job you want doing, and also look out for specific mentions of them tidying up after they finish their work – always a good indicator of a meticulous tradesperson." –Muna Nwokolo

When you're posting your job, make sure you provide as much information as you can – including photos, if possible. Of course, if you haven't seen the fault yourself, you'll need to ask your tenant for the information you need. At Yellow Lettings, we have an online system that walks the tenant step-by-step through questions that help us diagnose any given issue and encourages them to upload photos, but as an individual landlord this will need to be more of a manual process.

Once you've posted the job, your next actions will depend on the type of job…

If you can provide sufficient detail and the job is a very simple one, a tradesperson should be able to quote you a simple all-inclusive (parts and labour) price for doing the job without needing to take a look at it. Personally, I'd avoid anyone who wanted to charge for their time by the hour. I want to know what spend I'm committing to – and for very simple jobs they should be able to estimate the cost easily enough.

For routine maintenance like this, the cost is likely to be under £200, so I wouldn't bother getting multiple quotes: if someone has great reviews and seems confident about what they're doing, I'd rather get it fixed and move on with my life rather than shop around to save £20.

For bigger jobs with more variables (like re-laying a floor where nobody's sure what's underneath), or where you only know of the symptom but not the cause, a site visit will be necessary. Although it's a pain to arrange with your tenant, it's pretty much the only way.

Whatever the size of job, make sure that whoever you instruct:

- Has valid liability insurance (MyBuilder and similar sites check this for you – which is another benefit of using them)

- Is a member of any relevant trade bodies

- Is willing to provide you with an all-in "parts and labour" price after satisfying themselves as to the scope of the job (with a site visit, if necessary)

- Is available to complete the job in a timescale that's acceptable to you

Instructing the repair and checking the work

If your tenant waits in to meet the tradesperson without you being there, make sure you instruct the tradesperson in advance not to take instructions from the tenant: they just need to report back to you, and you will decide what gets done and when. If it's something that can potentially be sorted right away, you might ask them to call you from the property and get your permission to go ahead, thus saving another visit.

Once the work is done, you won't want to make payment until you've checked that the problem is fixed and the standard is acceptable – which you could accomplish by asking the trades-person to send you photos, asking the tenant, or going to see it yourself. If you're nearby and it's convenient, being there in person when the tradesperson is finishing up is ideal: you can point out anything they've missed and get them to put it right without having to wait for them to come back another time.

Try to get the work checked and approved as quickly as you can, so that you can pay the invoice with minimal delay: you've invested all this effort in finding a good tradesperson, so you want to pay quickly to ensure you stay in their good books. The hope is that when you next need them for a job, they'll do all they can to squeeze you in around their other commitments. Also, it's just the decent thing to do.

Pro tip: "I've got one local handyman who I feel never charges enough, so I usually give him a bit more – and I pay him promptly in person to say how pleased I am. I have to go out of my way, but having the relationship is well worth it." –Gareth Broom

Chapter 23

Dealing with routine maintenance issues

Every so often you'll have to deal with a real curveball of a maintenance issue, but thankfully the majority are boringly predictable – to the extent that you can be looking out for them before they happen. Remember: it's always quicker and cheaper to deal with an issue before it has a chance to become serious.

In this chapter we'll go over the most common maintenance issues, and what to do when you encounter them.

Pro tip: "Try to find a reliable 'odd job' man – they're worth their weight in gold. I found mine via a free advert on Gumtree. He will communicate directly with the tenant, and I'll just get a bill when it's done." –Mark Morris

Pro tip: "Always ask your tenant if they can fix the issue (for a rent reduction or similar), or if they know someone who might be able to fix the issue. I always tell my tenants that it's their home, and they should have a choice on who fixes things (within reason, of course)." –Kylie Ackers

Damp, mould and condensation

The most common tenant complaint you're going to receive is about "damp" – which is very often a result of how the tenant is using the property rather than something fundamentally wrong with the structure itself.

> *Pro tip: "Most tenants – and most landlords – don't understand the difference between damp and condensation, and 'damp' is the most common cause of complaints to Environmental Health. We give our tenants a fact sheet every September explaining how to care for the property, because the winter months are when complaints tend to occur." –Joanne Dron*

Most commonly, when a tenant reports damp it will actually be condensation – the symptoms of which can include the appearance of dark mould on the walls (especially around windows), water droplets on windows and walls, and an unpleasant smell.

Condensation will always happen to some degree (unless you can convince your tenants to leave the heating off and stop breathing), but it's made much worse by excessive moisture and poor ventilation. This often results from things like:

- Drying laundry indoors with the windows closed

- Cooking with the windows closed

- Taking hot showers with the windows closed

- Generally not opening the bloody windows!

While reassuring tenants and without sounding like you're dismissing their concerns, the best course of action is to have a conversation with them about how they can help to prevent problems by avoiding some of the behaviours above. Ask them to make these changes so you can eliminate them as possible causes – and if they're still experiencing problems with condensation after taking these measures, you'll need to look at what else can be done.

If it turns out that further action is needed, you can look at solutions like:

- Installing trickle vents in double-glazed windows (and making sure any existing vents aren't blocked)

- Installing extra air bricks in exterior walls to increase ventilation

- Using anti-mould paint in areas that are particularly susceptible to it

- Providing a dehumidifier

- Installing an extractor fan (or upgrading to a more powerful one) in the bathroom, and setting it to run for ten minutes after the light is turned off

Sometimes, rather than being condensation, reports of damp are caused by something more serious: rising damp or penetrating damp.

Rising damp is caused by ground water moving up through a wall or floor – and it often causes damage to skirting boards and low-level plaster. Penetrating damp is caused by water leaking through the walls (for example, if there's faulty guttering that regularly soaks the walls), and will show itself in the form of patches higher up the walls.

If you think you have either, you'll need to call in a damp-proofing company. The solution commonly involves removing all the old plaster (which will get dust *everywhere*), injecting a damp-proof substance into the wall and re-plastering – after which it will take six weeks to dry before you can re-paint the walls.

This is a real pain because it's not something a tenant is going to live through, so it'll have to wait until they move out. You'll also struggle to re-let the property while the walls are unpainted, so you'll be stuck with a void period. There's not much you can do about it, so just make sure rising or penetrating damp really *is* the cause before doing anything drastic.

No heating or hot water

Boilers do go wrong – and when they do, you'll need to get a plumber out to take a look (or get the tenant to call the relevant number, if you have boiler cover or emergency insurance).

But a lot of boiler faults are either user error or a simple fix that tenants can make themselves – avoiding a call-out fee. One common problem is the boiler losing pressure – so when they first report a lack of heating, ask them to read the pressure off the gauge on the boiler, and the boiler's manual will tell you what the pressure *should* be. If it's too low, it's then easy for them to fix it if you give them instructions (a link to a YouTube video usually does the trick). Do make them aware, though, that they should report if they're having to do it regularly, as it could indicate a leak or more serious fault.

To prevent anything more serious from happening, you could get the boiler serviced every year (which is frequently a condition of having boiler or emergency cover anyway). It can usually be done at the same time as the annual gas safety certificate for a small extra fee.

However diligent you are, sod's law dictates that you'll eventually have a boiler that terminally packs in over Christmas and New Year. For situations like this, you can buy some time and goodwill by having a stash of fan heaters ready to drop off when needed.

Washing machines

The easiest way to avoid washing machine dramas is not to provide one in the first place. But if that's not an option, make sure you know how to fix common issues so you can pass that information on to your tenants.

A common issue is the drain pump filter getting blocked – and tenants can do the small job of clearing it out themselves. Include the relevant page of the instruction manual in your house manual, and make tenants aware that they'll be charged for any call-outs that turn out to be just a blocked filter.

> Pro tip: "Find a make and model you're happy with – I use a midrange Bosch. You get to know the average period of use before you get an issue, and can then proactively plan to replace it before issues arise, or at least very quickly replace when the call comes through without the need to do any research. Also, Argos sells Bosch, will deliver the next day, and remove the old machine for you (for a little extra charge). Sorted!" –Matthew Webster

Other appliances

As with washing machines, the easiest way to deal with appliances is not to provide them in the first place. Even if they're not strictly "broken", they can still be an endless source of complaints: fridges and freezers can be "too cold" or "not cold enough", washing machines can be "too small" or "don't get my clothes as clean as my old one", or any number of other things.

If providing appliances can't be avoided (because you get feedback from prospective tenants that it's a deal breaker), draw your tenant's attention to the instruction manuals and read them yourself to see if there seems to be an easy fix for whatever they're trying to describe. Although you can tell them that they'll be charged for any call-outs that turn out to be due to their own misuse, it's far less hassle (and will generate less ill-feeling) if it can be avoided in the first place.

Pro tip: "Our ASTs usually contain a clause stating that while appliances are supplied, the landlord will remove any appliance (and not replace it) in the event of breakdown or failure to operate it in the desired manner.

Another option is to give the tenant money for a new appliance, an extra amount for delivery and a little additional for the 'inconvenience'. At the same time we get them to sign that the appliance is being removed from the inventory and is no longer the landlord's responsibility. The appliance is theirs to keep – even at the future point when they move out. This not only generates goodwill (because the tenant is being given a new appliance of their choice to keep), but also removes the future time it takes to deal with any issues." –Matt Elder

Leaks

A leak is a pain if it's happening inside your property, and can be an *enormous* pain if another flat in a block is leaking into yours.

If the leak is in your own property, turn off the water at the stopcock and call someone to come and investigate. If the stopcock is stuck beyond the point of just being a bit stiff, don't force it: if it breaks, you could flood the property and cause a lot of damage. Instead, call the water supplier and get them to come and investigate.

If the leak is clearly coming from a tap, appliance or toilet, you may be able to isolate the leak by turning off the service valve for just that piece of equipment. A quarter-turn with a flat-head screwdriver is enough to stop the water flowing and prevent any further damage.

You can include instructions in the house manual for how to take these simple measures – but you're more likely to have to explain them over the phone, as your tenant probably won't start leafing through the manual when there's water gushing through the ceiling.

If another flat is leaking into yours, you'll need to contact the block manager and get them to gain access to the flats above to find the source. Leaks normally come from directly above, but not necessarily – so it might take some time to gain access to several flats and eventually pin down the source.

Blocked drains

If a sink, bath or shower is draining slowly or not at all, make the tenants aware that this starts off as their responsibility: they should fish out any hair or other obstructions, and use a drain-unblocking product.

You should instruct a plumber if it turns out to be anything more serious, of course, but make clear that the tenants will be charged for the visit if they haven't done their bit first.

Pests

Infestations of pests – including mice, rats, bed bugs, wasps, bats and more – aren't much fun to live with, and can be more expensive to evict than tenants are.

The first thing to do is establish who is responsible for dealing with them – which can be tricky. If you've got a clause in your tenancy agreement (as recommended) saying that it's the tenant's responsibility, that's helpful – but there can still be grey areas.

For example, if mice are getting access through holes in the external wall, you have a statutory responsibility to make sure that the structure of the building is sound. But in reality, mice can get through a hole the size of a 10p piece – and it's just not practical to have every minuscule hole totally blocked up. It's especially tricky if the kitchen is filthy with crumbs and leftover food everywhere, in which case you could argue that it's the tenant's fault for creating such a mouse-friendly environment.

In the first instance, I'd recommend reminding the tenant that dealing with pests is their responsibility under the tenancy agreement – and only get involved if an inspection reveals that there's a clear structural defect that's allowing access.

This doesn't apply if tenants report a problem with pests as soon as they move in: this implies that the pests were present from the start, and it's therefore not the tenant's responsibility. In this case, you'll have to treat the infestation yourself.

Pro tip: "Try the local council first: they often have their own dedicated team that's cheaper than using a private firm." –Nathan Browne

Chapter 24

Conducting inspections

It's a good idea, if at all practical, to visit the property every six months to check on its general condition. This isn't a full inventory like you'd conduct at the start of a tenancy, but just an opportunity to check that the tenant is treating the property responsibly and there are no major items of maintenance that haven't been reported.

At Yellow Lettings, we conduct an initial visit after six weeks (because if something tenant-related is going to go wrong, it generally happens early and we can nip it in the bud), and thereafter every six months.

> Pro tip: "Use regular inspections to check on external issues like making sure the guttering is clear, as tenants generally won't notice or report problems like this until they're affecting them seriously." –Jo Lines

The tenant can be present for inspections or not, but either way the visit should be presented to them as a chance to look for anything that might need sorting out for them – *not* an excuse to come into their home and judge their behaviour. And just like any other type of visit to the property, the tenant needs to have at least 24 hours' written notice of your intention to visit – which they're free to decline.

Inspections are quick and easy to do yourself if you want to, but inventory clerks will also be willing to conduct inspections if you don't have the time or confidence to do it yourself.

How to conduct an inspection

Rather than just wander around and see what you see, you should create a template for making room-by-room notes. You're really just recording general observations and taking any supporting photographs that are necessary – not moving furniture, opening cupboards and being as detailed as you would be for an inventory.

(If you're not doing the inspection yourself, it will be helpful to provide a copy of the most recent inventory to the person doing the inspection: it'll allow them to cross-reference and see whether the condition of an item has significantly deteriorated since the start of the tenancy.)

Look carefully around each room to check for anything that could be repaired or replaced to improve safety or just provide the tenant with better living conditions. For example, if a piece of carpet at the top of the stairs has come loose, that's something worth recording and correcting right away. Don't forget to also look at the exterior of the building.

Also look for signs of condensation (so you can advise the tenant about how they can stop it from getting worse), and any areas where it appears that they're using the property in a way that could result in damage – such as overloading electrical sockets.

If you spot anything likely to cause damage to the property, you have the right to insist that it's put right quickly: put in writing what needs to be done, and arrange a re-inspection once they've had a reasonable amount of time to fix it.

> Pro tip: "However lovely your place is, cover your eyes, stick your fingers in your ears and sing when you see how the tenants are keeping it. It will always need a lick of paint and some love before you re-let, so don't sweat it." –Richard Taylor

Once the inspection is complete, sign and date it and ask the tenant to do the same (either in person or over email), then file it away with the tenancy agreement and other paperwork.

Other things to look out for

While you're there, you can take the opportunity to:

- Test any smoke detectors

- Look out for any fire risks arising from tenant behaviour, like overloaded electrical sockets or tea towels left on the hob

- Check for obvious evidence (without going through

tenants' possessions) of unauthorised pets or more occupants than are listed on the tenancy agreement

And that's it for inspections! They don't have to be an arduous task, and they're extremely useful in helping you spot potential issues early – before they have a chance to become more serious.

Chapter 25

Renewing the tenancy

If the original fixed-term tenancy is nearing its end and the tenants want to stay, you'll need to mutually decide on one of two different options to extend the arrangement.

The first is to set up another fixed-term tenancy. Assuming nothing else has changed, this is as simple as printing another copy of your existing agreement with new dates and having all parties sign it. An extension of 6 or 12 months is typical.

The second is to do nothing, and have the tenancy continue on a periodic basis. As we saw in Part 3, when a fixed term ends, the tenancy automatically continues and becomes periodic – with the period being the same as the frequency of rental demands. That means if the rent is paid monthly, the agreement continues month-to-month and the tenant just needs to give one month's notice to end the agreement. (The landlord still needs to give two months' notice in this scenario, as we'll see in Part 5.)

Which is the right thing to do? It depends: signing up for another fixed term gives both parties security, whereas leaving it periodic gives both parties flexibility. As a landlord, you may also want to consider timing: for example, if your property is in an area with strong student demand, you might want to make sure renewals always come up at the time of the year when students are most actively looking. In this situation, you might *not* want to leave the tenancy to become periodic because the tenant could then end it at the wrong time of year for you to be marketing it again.

There's no "right" answer, but the option you choose has important implications for your power to both increase the rent and end the tenancy. We'll explore these implications fully in the next couple of chapters, but I wanted to mention the issue of renewal now because it's an important part of managing a tenancy: make a note in your diary for a few months before the tenancy is due to end, because then you'll have plenty of time to decide what you want to do and come to an agreement with your tenants.

Chapter 26

Increasing the rent

The rental market is changing all the time, and if market rents in the area have gone up significantly since your tenant moved in, you might consider increasing the rent to a level that's still competitive for the area. As we'll see, there are several mechanisms for you to do this.

But *should* you do it? This is where honest communication with the tenant comes in.

If the rent increase you're proposing is fair, talk to the tenant and explain why you want to do it. You can even point to examples of comparable properties nearby that are asking for more than they're currently paying. This accomplishes two things. First, it shows that you're not just trying your luck. Second, it implies that if they leave they'll probably end up paying the higher rent anyway (because what you're asking for is fair for the market).

Approach this as a negotiation, and try to make the tenant feel like they're getting something out of the deal – after all, nobody likes to be told they have to pay more for the same level of service. You might agree that in exchange for the rent increase, you'll provide a new cooker or replace a carpet that's starting to look a bit tatty. (You *can't*, however, hold the tenant to ransom and refuse to make essential repairs unless they pay more!)

Is the tenant still unwilling or unable to pay the extra? Then you have to decide whether to keep the rent as it is or ask them to leave and find a new tenant who's willing to pay. This decision will come down to two factors.

Firstly, financial: how long will it take you to find a new tenant, and are there any cosmetic (non-essential) improvements you'll need to make before you can do so? If the property is empty for a month while you look for a tenant and the increase you wanted was £50 per month, it could take you over a year to recoup the lost rent from the void period with the increased rent you're charging – and the new tenant might not even stay for that long. Remember too that this isn't even taking into account your time and effort in *finding* the new tenant (think back to everything you had to do in Parts 2 and 3!).

Secondly, the slightly less tangible: is your current tenant a good tenant? If they don't cause any hassle, take good care of the property and pay their rent on time every month, there's a value that's hard to put a figure on. How do you rate your chances of finding another tenant like that?

If, after thinking all this through, you *do* decide to increase the rent, how you do so will depend on where in the lifecycle of the tenancy you are.

When a fixed term ends

During the initial fixed term of a tenancy, you can't increase the rent at all – *unless* the increase was written into the tenancy agreement in the first place.

For example, if your tenancy agreement is for 12 months and there's a clause stating that the rent will increase by £50 per month after the first six months, that's fine. But if there's no such mention and you decide you want to make an increase after six months anyway, no dice.

It's more typical to negotiate an increase in rent when a fixed term comes to an end. At this point you can do one of the following:

- Agree with the tenant to sign a new tenancy agreement for another fixed term (6 or 12 months), with a different level of rent.

- Allow the current agreement to continue on a "periodic" basis as we've discussed before, but agree an amendment to the level of rent stated in the contract.

The option you choose will depend on the trade-off between security and flexibility that you both want. It could be that the tenant doesn't want to commit beyond the next few months, and you're fine with that. Alternatively, they might be anxious to sign up for another year because they've got a child in a nearby school and don't want to move. Either way, a couple of months before the fixed term is due to end, start the conversation about what to do next – and make the level of rent part of that discussion if you do want to increase it.

During a periodic tenancy

Once the fixed term is over and the tenancy is continuing on a periodic basis, there are three ways in which you can increase the rent.

The first way is to look at what's written in the tenancy agreement. If there's a clause stating that the rent will increase by a certain percentage (or in line with RPI inflation) if the tenancy continues beyond a year, for example, then that's settled: what is written is what will happen, and the tenant agreed when they signed the initial contract so they can't argue with it.

If there isn't a clause in the agreement about rent increases, that still leaves you with two options.

The first is to mutually agree the increase with the tenants. If they agree, you simply need to get this agreement in writing and signed by both parties. There's no set format to this document: you should just write down what's been agreed and attach it to the tenancy agreement as documentary evidence in case you need it later.

If the tenant *doesn't* agree, you can still attempt to force through an increase by issuing a Section 13 notice. This notice does need to have specific wording on it to be valid, and you can download a template from the gov.uk website: search "assured tenancy forms", and you need Form 4.

A Section 13 notice needs to be issued at least one month before the rent rise is to come into effect, assuming that the rent is paid monthly or weekly. If the tenant thinks that the new level of rent is unacceptable, they can refer the case to a Rent Assessment Committee.

In practice, though, Section 13 is very seldom used: if a tenant isn't happy to mutually agree a higher level of rent (and the new rent you're asking for is reasonable given local market conditions), it probably makes more sense to end the tenancy rather than go through the whole legal process and have a resentful tenant on your hands. If the new rent you want to charge is reasonable, it shouldn't be a problem to find someone else who's willing to pay it. (And if it's not reasonable, you shouldn't be trying your luck!)

Conclusion to Part 4

Although this section contained a lot of scary stuff about emergencies and missing rent, I hope you've still come away with the impression that property management isn't overly daunting. The key is to be proactive to prevent issues from arising in the first place, and to act quickly if they still do. Acting fast is always cheapest and makes for happier tenants who stay longer.

This is where a good managing agent has great value, too. If you're just not able to react quickly or visit the property somewhat regularly (maybe because you work long hours or live a long way from the property), paying a managing agent will actually *save* you money because they'll notice problems early (before they become serious) and keep your tenant happy. (A not-so-good managing agent will do none of these things but take your money anyway, so in the bonus chapters I'll show you how to choose a good one.)

So that's the tenancy chugging nicely along, and long may it do so. At some point, though, either you or the tenant will want to bring the tenancy to an end – so in Part 5 I'll cover how to manage that situation.

PART 5:
ENDING THE TENANCY

Introduction

All good things – including tenancies – must come to an end.

Despite the horror stories you've no doubt heard, 90% of tenancies simply end as a result of the tenant making the decision to move on. This leaves you with work to do – like conducting a check-out and sorting out any deductions from the deposit – but as long as you've done everything correctly up to this point, it's relatively straightforward.

Then there's the other 10% of cases: where you want to take the property back to move back in, sell it, or get a rent increase that your current tenants won't pay… or the rare-but-nasty situation of having to evict the tenant because they turned the bedroom into a meth lab and used the garden for satanic rituals involving bunny rabbits.

We'll cover it all in this section – starting with the most easy and common situation, and building our strength to tackle the tough stuff…

Chapter 27

When tenants give notice to leave

If you're upset rather than jumping for joy when your tenants say they want to leave, that's a good thing: it means you'll have had a positive relationship with them, and they've treated your property well.

Upset you may be, but it's your responsibility to help them make the move as smoothly as possible. Tenants (quite reasonably) often have a limited understanding of how the end of a tenancy actually works, and this chapter will help you understand it yourself so you can better help them.

Before we start, though, it's worth pointing out that you don't *have* to follow the legal requirement exactly. Say your tenant wants to be let out of a contract early and that suits you too... anything you both agree between you can supersede what's written in the tenancy agreement.

So, when can tenants give notice to leave?

At a break clause during the fixed term

If the tenancy agreement has a break clause, the tenant can execute it by following the procedure that's written in the tenancy agreement in terms of how much notice should be given and so on.

There's no standard form of break clause, so you and the tenant should both refer to the agreement to see exactly how it should work.

Before the end of the fixed term

It happens: a tenant signs an agreement for a 12-month tenancy without a break clause, then has a change of circumstance (or just of heart) after six months and wants to leave.

In this situation, you'd be entirely within your rights to hold them to the full term of the tenancy – so they can move out if they want to, but they would need to keep paying you rent right up until the end of the term that was originally agreed.

This is almost never a good idea, though: you'll either have resentful tenants in your property who don't want to be there and aren't motivated to look after it, or they'll stop paying rent and you'll have to go through the courts to get it back.

It's far better to come to a compromise: ask them to pay your costs for remarketing the property, and you'll release them from their agreement as soon as replacement tenants are ready to move in.

This allows them to get (almost) what they want, without leaving you financially worse off. Helpfully, this also means your interests are aligned so they're likely to be bending over backwards to accommodate viewings and keeping the place in tiptop condition for when people come round.

At the end of the fixed term

Tenancy agreements tend to require that the tenant gives at least one month's notice of their intention to leave – whether that's at the end of the fixed term or at some later date once the tenancy has become periodic.

(Under the Housing Act, a tenant is actually allowed to just move out on the last day of a fixed term without giving any notice whatsoever: the final day is the one and only day when they can legitimately do this. In practice this is unusual, and tenants will generally abide by the contractual notice requested in the tenancy agreement.)

So if your agreement states that one month's notice must be given and your tenant gives their notice two weeks before the fixed term is due to end, you're within your rights to hold them to a full month – and take the extra couple of weeks' rent from their deposit if necessary. But of course, you don't have to: the agreement may insist on a month, but you can be nice and accept a shorter amount of time if you want to.

During a periodic tenancy

Once a fixed term has ended and the tenancy has been continuing on a "periodic" basis, the tenant can give notice of their intention to leave by giving one period's notice. If the period (as defined by the frequency that the rent is paid) is monthly, that means a month's notice – and if the period is quarterly, it means a quarter. But if it's weekly, then the notice period is longer: 28 days.

It's not the case, however, that they can just give a month's notice starting from whenever they feel like it: the final "leaving" date must also coincide with the last day of a period.

As an example:

- The rent is paid monthly, so the period is one month.

- The rent is paid on the 1st of the month.

- The tenant contacts you on 5th March wanting to leave.

The earliest that the tenant could leave in this situation (contacting you on 5th March) would be 30th April. This is because they're too late to give a whole period's notice and still leave on the day before the rent is next due (31st March).

This isn't particularly intuitive for tenants and there's no reason why they should know this, so you'll probably have to explain all this when they let you know of their intention to leave you. Although, as I said, if they want to leave earlier than 30th April and it suits you for them to do so, there's no reason why you shouldn't agree an earlier date between you.

How should a tenant give notice to leave?

The tenancy agreement will state how the tenant is to give notice, which will normally involve writing to the landlord's address that's provided on the tenancy agreement.

Again, though, you don't have to insist on this: if the tenant notifies you by email and you're happy with that, you don't have to push for a letter unless you want to. It is, however, a good idea to get it in writing rather than just have them tell you verbally (to avoid potential misunderstandings later).

Chapter 28

Asking tenants to leave

When the tenant wants to leave, it's a relatively straightforward process – as we've just seen. But what if it's *you* who wants to end the tenancy?

In this chapter we'll look in some detail at how to end a tenancy for a reason *other than a tenant's bad behaviour* – which could include:

- You want the property back to live in yourself.

- You want to increase the rent, and the tenant is unable or unwilling to pay more.

- You want to sell the property.

When can you ask tenants to leave?

As we now know, a tenancy has a fixed term (often 6 or 12 months), after which it can either end, be renewed for another fixed term, or automatically continue as a "periodic" tenancy.

Unless there's a break clause in the tenancy agreement, you

can't end the tenancy *during* the fixed term except in specific circumstances. These circumstances usually relate to a *very bad thing* happening (like the tenant being seriously behind with their rent), and we'll deal with that in the "Eviction" chapter.

So if you can't end a tenancy *during* a fixed term, there are two times when you can:

- At the end of the fixed term

- When the fixed term has been over for a while, and the tenancy has been continuing on a "periodic" basis

Giving the right amount of notice

OK, let's imagine your tenants have signed a year-long tenancy agreement with you. After they've been living there eight months, you decide (for reasons unrelated to their conduct) that you'd like to take the property back at the end of the fixed term.

(Maybe you'd ideally have the property back *before* the end of the fixed term – but, as we've just discussed, you can't do that unless there are particular circumstances related to the tenant's behaviour. We'll explore those circumstances in the "Eviction" chapter.)

What you need to do is serve something called a **Section 21 notice**. This is just a form that gives your tenant legal notice that you want to take the property back and they need to be out by a certain date. Essentially, it's just saying "Look, you've done nothing wrong and I'm sure you're a lovely person, but I need this property back." The words "lovely person" don't appear anywhere in the prescribed wording of a Section 21 notice, but you get the idea: this is a "no fault" process.

Of all the statutory notices in the Housing Act, Section 21 should be your favourite (wait, doesn't everyone have a favourite statutory instrument?). That's because if you complete the procedure correctly, there's nothing that can go wrong: even if the tenants fail to leave when they're supposed to, the court process to remove them is (relatively) quick and there's no danger of a judge overturning what you're trying to do.

So, how do you serve a Section 21 notice correctly? Well, first, you need to make sure you've *already* complied with various tenancy rules:

- You need to have a valid Assured Shorthold Tenancy, with the tenancy agreement being in writing (which you will do if you followed everything in Part 3).

- You should be able to prove that you've complied with all deposit-related legislation and provided your tenant with the necessary paperwork (again, Part 3 has you covered).

- You should have provided the tenant with all the documents we also ran through in Part 3 – namely the gas safety certificate, EPC and (in England) "How to rent" leaflet.

- You can't have received an Improvement Notice from the local authority as a result of your failure to make essential repairs in a reasonable period of time.

- Your tenancy must have run for at least six months. There's no reason why you can't have a tenancy agreement that's only intended to last (say) three months, but the courts won't award possession under Section 21 unless the tenancy is at least six months old.

If you have all that covered, it's on to the next steps for a correct and successful Section 21:

- Fill in the right form, and do it correctly (more on this in the next section).

- Give at least two months' notice of your intention to take the property back on a certain date.

  The key here is giving sufficient notice – which must be at least two months, but can be more. So:

  - The tenancy started on 11th June 2015.

  - You decide in January 2016 that you want the property back at the end of the fixed term.

  - You issue a Section 21 notice stating that you want the property back at the end of 10th June 2016.

The same procedure applies if you decide right towards the end of the tenancy that you want to get possession back. For example, when the tenancy only has a month left to run, you realise that you want it back – but as you need to give at least two months' notice, you can't request possession on the last day of the fixed term. That's fine: just serve the notice giving two months' notice, and the tenancy will effectively continue on a periodic basis for one month after the fixed term before you take it back. So:

- The tenancy started on 11th June 2015.

- On 1st May 2016 you decide that you want the property back ASAP.

- You serve a Section 21 notice stating that you want the property back at the end of 1st July 2016 (after the end of the fixed term, and giving two months' notice).

And the same goes for if the fixed term has already ended and the tenancy is periodic. Continuing the example, you might decide on 4th September 2016 that you want to get the property back. Not a problem: as long as the tenancy hasn't been renewed, you can serve notice to get the property back on 4th November 2016.

(Quick note: the requirements around dates are slightly different for tenancies that started before 1 October 2015, but we won't get into that here because I'm assuming you're reading this book with a view to managing a tenancy that hasn't started yet.)

Once again, what we're talking about here is only what you must do legally to be able to get possession – and if you agree something different with your tenants, that's fine. So in this case, if you give two months' notice but the tenants are actually happy to move out early and you're happy with that too, there's no reason why that can't happen.

How to write and serve a Section 21 notice

So, what is a Section 21 notice – and how does one "serve" a notice in the first place?

Well, firstly it has to be in writing, and it's best served by post or in person because these methods give clear-cut ways of proving that you've done so. If you serve a notice by First Class post, it's deemed to be "served" on the second business day after posting. If you serve it in person (by posting it through the door or putting it in the tenant's hand), it's deemed to be served that day if you deliver it before 4.30pm (as long as it's a business day) or the next business day if it's after 4.30pm.

Whichever method you choose, it's a good idea to have proof: a certificate of postage if sending by post, or a time-stamped photograph of you posting it through the door if you're hand-delivering. *Don't* use a method that requires a signature, because the tenant can refuse delivery or it can be sent back to the depot if they're not home.

That established, it's on to the notice itself. You'll be needing to use good old DCLG Form 6a, which you can download from www.propertygeek.net/6a

It's surprisingly easy: print, fill in the blanks, and send. There you go: you've just instigated a Section 21 procedure.

What if the tenant refuses to leave?

So, the date on the Section 21 comes and goes, but the tenant doesn't. Go, that is. What do you do?

You can't do a DIY eviction job, but provided you've done everything correctly, you can use the "accelerated possession procedure" to get the courts to legally remove the tenant. This involves filling in a form, sending it off to your local court with all relevant documentation, and paying a fee (which at the time of writing is £280). You can start the process online here: www.gov.uk/accelerated-possession-eviction

You don't need to turn up to court: provided everything has been done correctly and the tenant can't mount a sensible de-fence, the court will be happy with the evidence you posted and issue a "possession order" without needing to hear any more from you – basically telling the tenant that they *seriously* need to leave now.

If they don't... no, you still can't apply any force yourself. You need to go back to the court again and ask their bailiffs to evict the tenant. You'll have to pay a bailiff fee and wait for a date when they're available – which you'll be notified of by post (as will your tenant). When that day arrives, you or a representative will need to attend with the bailiffs – and you'll probably find that the tenant has finally, after all that hassle, gone. (A letter from the bailiff tends to have that effect on people.)

If the tenant *hasn't* gone already, the bailiffs will make sure they're finally forced out – and you can change the locks.

This process isn't cheap, fun or quick – which is why Rent Guarantee Insurance (which often covers the legal costs of eviction and pays rent up until the point that the property is empty) can be attractive. If you don't have insurance like this, it's extremely important that your emergency fund contains enough to meet your mortgage and other expenses for the several months that it might take for the possession process to go through the courts. (And, of course, you still need extra in your fund for all the "normal" stuff too – like repairs.)

Don't panic!

This has been a long and detailed chapter, but that doesn't mean you'll have to worry about this sort of thing happening often. If you've picked a good tenant, you'll ask them to leave and they'll leave: you'll still issue a Section 21 notice, but they're not going to hang on by the fingernails while the bailiffs try to force them out of the door, or try to get the case thrown out of court on a technicality.

You've almost certainly heard war stories from landlords or

watched TV shows about tenants refusing to leave – but the reason they make good pub story or TV fodder is because they're relatively rare. That's why I put so much emphasis on choosing a good tenant: you can never be sure, but if you get that part right, you should (fingers crossed) never have to go through a protracted legal process to get the property back.

But what if you need to evict the tenant for reasons other than wanting the property back? What if, say, they've decided that they'd "rather not" pay the rent anymore – or that your newly painted cream walls look more interesting when they've been graffitied up a bit? Then things *can* get nasty, and we'll work our way through that scenario shortly. First, though, we'll complete the process you'll go through in the "normal" situation of the tenancy ending when no one's at fault.

Chapter 29

Moving tenants out

With the formalities out of the way, it's time to move on to the practicalities of bringing the tenancy to an end. You'll be conducting a check-out and arranging the return of the tenants' deposit, and – unless you're taking back the property to sell, refurbish or live in yourself – you'll want to start lining up their replacements at the same time too.

Reducing gaps between tenancies

Whether it was you or your tenants who initiated the end of the tenancy, you'll want to turn the property around quickly – to minimise the gap between tenancies when you're not collecting any rent and you become liable for any bills.

By following everything in this book so far, you'll have put yourself in a good position: you'll have good photos you can use to start marketing the property, you'll have been inspecting regularly so you know anything that's likely to need attention before your new tenants move in, and you'll have a team of tradespeople ready to get straight on the case.

The challenge, typically, is getting access for viewings – and when you do have access, making sure the property isn't in a state that repels potential tenants.

Most tenancy agreements will have a clause stating that the tenants should give access for viewings during the last month of the tenancy, but this is very difficult to enforce in practice. Nobody wants strangers tramping through their property every evening, especially if they're trying to get everything packed up and ready to move on, so tenants can be difficult about allowing viewings. There's nothing you can do to force them, other than gently referring them to what it says in their tenancy agreement and maybe subtly reminding them that you'll be giving a reference to their next landlord.

Then once you *do* have access, the property isn't going to show as well as it did when it was empty, clean and tidy. It might take more viewings to re-let than it did to let it in the first place, because potential tenants will have to see past any mess and it'll be harder for them to imagine it feeling like their own home.

There's no easy answer to any of this – other than to have a good relationship with your tenants. If you're on good terms, you can explain why having viewings is important to you, and work with them to choose a few convenient times for block viewings to minimise disruption. Then when you have those viewings, arrive early to make sure the place looks presentable: you can't go around moving all your tenants' possessions, but simple things like opening curtains, straightening bedding and hiding dirty plates will make a big difference.

As noted earlier, it's easier if it was the tenants who gave notice to leave and they ideally want to be out earlier than their notice period allows. You don't *have* to accept a shorter notice period, but you could say that you'll allow them out of the agreement as soon as a tenant has been found to replace them. They'll therefore be amenable about viewings in order to get out early, and this will work in your favour too because you'll be likely to have a shorter gap than if you forced them to stay until the end.

If all has gone well, you could have new tenants ready to move in before the previous ones have left – and there's nothing to stop you from going through the referencing process and having everything lined up for them to be handed the keys the moment the property becomes empty. Just *stop short of actually signing the tenancy agreement* with the new tenants: while uncommon, it's not beyond the realms of possibility that the current tenants will have a last-minute change of heart (if it was them who ended the tenancy) or suddenly refuse to go as planned (if it was you). If you haven't signed the tenancy agreement, you'll still have to let down the new tenants and refund them all their money – but at least there's no opening for them to pursue you for breach of contract.

In almost every case, though, everything will go as planned and you'll be able to check the tenants out – although before you do, there are steps you can take to help the tenancy end smoothly.

Before the check-out

In the last month of the tenancy, it's your responsibility to get in touch with your tenants and make them aware of what they need to do before the tenancy comes to an end.

If it's been a while since your last inspection, you could plan one during the last month to check the condition of the property and make them aware of anything that will need to be rectified in order for them to get their deposit back in full.

Whether you visit the property or not, you should let them know that they have the following responsibilities:

- Leave the property in the same state in which they found it, in terms of tidiness and cleanliness – and with no items missing if the property was furnished (it might be helpful to give them a copy of the inventory to compare against, in case they can't find their copy)

- Dispose of any of their own furniture or belongings that they won't be taking with them (they shouldn't just leave them at the property for you to deal with)

- Make sure they have the same number of keys to return as they were given

- Arrange the cancellation of any contracts with telephone or internet companies

- Arrange for their post to be forwarded with the Royal

Mail, if required

- Make sure all lightbulbs are working

- Provide you with their new address so you can contact them regarding any final matters

- Pay the utility bills up to the final day of the tenancy

You should also find out from the tenants when they're planning on leaving – as it may be before the final date of the tenancy. Tenants have the right to be present at the check-out, but they don't have to be: it's generally less confrontational for them *not* to be present, as long as they've been given fair warning of what's expected of them in terms of cleanliness and preparation.

At the check-out

This is where your inventory comes into its own, as it's the document you'll be referring back to in order to establish whether (with the exception of fair wear and tear) everything is in the same condition as it was when the tenancy started.

(In the next chapter, we'll look at how to establish what counts as "fair wear and tear" and what counts as damage – and in the case of damage, how much you can reasonably deduct from the deposit.)

Just like the check-in and any inspections, the check-out report can be done by you or delegated to a professional inventory clerk. Whoever does it, all that's required is to go through the property while noting:

- Anything that's damaged or broken

- Anything listed on the inventory that isn't present any-more

- Anything that *isn't* on the inventory, which tenants appear to be leaving behind

- Anything that's not in an acceptable state of cleanliness

As ever, take photos (or even video) to support what you notice.

At the same time:

- Make sure all the keys are returned

- Take readings of the gas and electricity meters (and water meter if present)

And that's that.

After the check-out

As soon as the tenants move out, you should contact the utility companies with the final meter readings, forwarding address for the tenants, and the details of the new occupier (which may be you, if the property is going to be empty for more than a few days before new tenants move in). You should also let the council know about the new occupier for council tax purposes.

You'd be amazed how much hassle can be avoided by notifying the council and utility companies at the beginning and end of the tenancy: it ensures that if a tenant leaves without paying their bills, those bills are clearly their responsibility because there's no doubt about when they lived there.

So with that taken care of, we can move on to the final (and very important) piece of admin: agreeing on the return of the tenants' deposit.

Chapter 30

Returning the deposit

Dealing with deposits isn't anyone's idea of fun, and it's often a major bone of contention between landlords and tenants. It can also be a massive time-suck: our first employee at Yellow Lettings joined us from a previous agency where her entire role involved handling disagreements about deposits.

But if you do everything right at the start of the tenancy and communicate well throughout it, you can significantly reduce the likelihood of having a disagreement. (And if there *is* a disagreement, it'll be far more likely that the decision will go in your favour if you turn to arbitration.) In this chapter, we'll cover all the main issues you need to be aware of.

Timescales

You need to release the deposit within ten days of agreeing any deductions to be made from it, and you can do so online using the website of whichever scheme provider you used.

If the entire deposit is being returned or the tenant has already agreed with you about the deductions that should be made, that's it: job done. And because it's so easy compared to the dispute resolution process (as we'll see in a minute), it's *always* worth trying to resolve any disagreements directly with your tenants. That's why it's a good idea to make an inspection during the month before the tenants leave, so you can tell them exactly what they need to do for them to get their full deposit back.

If you end up disagreeing with them over £50, you might even decide to be pragmatic and gracefully back down: the time you spend fighting over it will take up far more than £50 of your time.

We'll soon cover what to do if you can't come to an agreement – but first, let's look at what deductions you might want to make from a deposit.

Cleanliness

One of the most common causes of disagreement about the return of deposits is cleaning – with tenants often claiming that the landlord hits them with a huge cleaning fee regardless of the condition in which they left the property.

To avoid disagreements about degrees of dirtiness, it's helpful – as I mentioned earlier – to conduct a full professional clean before letting a property for the first time. That way, it's clear that the first tenants need to give it back in the same spotless condition – and assuming they do give it back similarly sparkling, there's no need to have it cleaned again before the next tenants move in. (You can't insist that the tenants themselves have the property professionally cleaned before they leave, but you can require that it's done "to a professional standard" – as long as that was the standard when they moved in.)

And if they don't clean to that standard before handing the property back? Then it's reasonable to deduct the cost of a professional clean if it's needed – although if only selected items are dirty (like the oven), it's only fair to charge for the cleaning of those items alone, and give the tenant the opportunity to come back and clean it to avoid the charge completely.

Damage or wear and tear?

As a landlord, you can only claim the costs of items that have been specifically damaged – not those that have degraded as a result of "fair wear and tear". A simple example is that a carpet becoming worn in the hallway is wear and tear, but a cigarette burn is damage.

What's considered "fair" wear and tear depends on the length of the tenancy and who the occupiers are. For example, you wouldn't expect a single professional to totally wear out a sofa within six months, but you might expect it if a whole family has been there for five years.

There are many occasions where the lines can get very blurred: are small marks on a light carpet fair enough or not? And what if *some* marks were present at the start but now there are more? This is why detailed photographs should form part of the inventory to avoid the vagaries of wording, but even *with* photos there are some issues that are going to come down to a judgement call – either by you in the first place, or the adjudicator if there's a dispute.

Calculating the cost of damage

Deductions for damaged items aren't an exact science, and will need to be negotiated between you and the tenant (with the deposit protection scheme – as we'll see in a minute – having the final say if you can't agree). Broadly, though, there are three types of expense that might result from a damaged item:

Cleaning. If there are stains all over a fabric sofa but a professional cleaning company could get these out, the appropriate amount to deduct would be whatever the cleaning company says they'll charge you.

Repair. Again, relatively straightforward: if a shelf has been ripped off the wall, you can charge the reasonable cost that a handyman would charge to put it back up and make good any damage to the plaster.

Sometimes damage can't be properly repaired, but it's not significant enough to replace the entire item. For example, you can't remove a burn mark from a work surface but it doesn't warrant ripping the whole thing out and starting again. In situations like this, the compensation can't help but be somewhat arbitrary – so landlords will often just apply charges like

£50 per mark.

It's a tricky situation: as a tenant I wouldn't want to be charged hundreds of pounds because of one mark, but as a landlord it does leave you with a property that looks significantly more shabby for incoming tenants and you're only able to claim a small amount. Unfortunately, it's just one of those things – which is why you'll inevitably have to budget for "cyclical works" (like repainting every few years), which won't be covered by deductions from anyone's deposit.

Replacement. Now things get really tricky – and a bit mathematical just to rub it in. If an item needs to be completely replaced as the result of damage, you can't just charge for the entire cost of a brand new replacement. Why? Because this would result in "betterment": if the tenant had been using a carpet for two years, you'd expect to have a slightly aged carpet at the end of the tenancy. But if they wrecked it and you replaced it, you'd end up with a brand new one. This would be a better situation than the slightly aged carpet you'd have had if they hadn't been so cavalier with their carpet usage, hence "betterment".

So, instead, the fair thing to do (and what would be done if the deposit protection scheme stepped in to adjudicate) is to calculate how much the item's lifespan had been foreshortened by their carelessness, and charge them for that portion. So, for example:

- Cost of a brand new carpet of the same quality: £500

- Age of carpet at the end of the tenancy: 2 years

- Average lifespan of a carpet with normal usage: 10 years

- Depreciation per year (new cost divided by total lifespan): £50

- Years of usage that would have remained if not damaged: 8 years

- Charge made (years foreshortened x annual depreciation): £400

Dispute resolution

What if you and the tenant just point-blank disagree about how much of the deposit should be retained, and no number of increasingly tetchy emails can break the deadlock? At this point, both parties are entitled to call in a third party adjudicator.

Each deposit protection scheme operates an "Alternative Dispute Resolution" (ADR) service (the "alternative" being to the courts), which impartially considers the evidence and decides whether the proposed deductions from a deposit are fair. The dispute process can be started online by either you or the tenant, and while the process is slightly different for each scheme, it should take no more than 60 days from start to finish.

Depending on the scheme, you'll often need to release any "undisputed" portion of the deposit to the tenants immediately, and transfer the disputed portion to the scheme to hold (if it's been in your own bank account up until now).

The adjudicator starts from the position that the deposit is the tenants' money, and the onus is on the landlord to prove any deductions that should be made. To do this, they consider evidence that's submitted by both sides – and after making their decision, it can only be challenged through the courts.

The most important evidence the adjudicator will consider is the tenancy agreement, the inventory and the check-out report, along with the photographic evidence that forms part of it. You'll be required to put a case forward by calling their attention to "before and after" photographs of the defects you're claiming, along with a justification for the deduction you want to make for it. You might also need to supply receipts or invoices for replacements or quotes for repairs.

What if you can't contact the tenant?

If you want to make a deduction from the deposit but the tenant has just disappeared and won't communicate with you about it, you can feel free to just keep the entire deposit.

Just kidding: *of course* it's not that easy! Instead you'll need to follow something called the Single Claims Process. This involves sending a "statutory declaration" to the deposit protection scheme you've been using, which you'll need to have stamped by a Solicitor, Commissioner for Oaths or Magistrate. Just like you would do normally, you need to state any deductions you want to make and how you've arrived at that figure. At this point, the scheme will take over and write to both parties. Either the tenant will respond (by agreeing, or disagreeing and triggering the dispute resolution process), or not – meaning that you "win".

The process to follow for the Single Claims Process will vary slightly depending on the scheme you use, but you'll find exact guidance on their website.

Summary

Deductions from deposits are a tricky subject. I'd argue that the situation is much fairer on tenants than it was pre-2007 – when no legislation existed and landlords could do basically whatever they wanted – and that's a good thing. But there are always going to be disputes and unfair situations sometimes, even when there's a detailed inventory.

As I said at the start of this chapter, the key is communication: tenants are far less likely to kick up a fuss if they're warned early about potential deductions and given the chance to refute them or put them right. You can imagine how you'd feel as a tenant if you'd never heard any complaints from your landlord about anything, then you suddenly got hit with a huge deduction from your deposit: it'd look like the landlord was just trying their luck, and you'd be more likely to contest it. Agreement without recourse to ADR is better for everyone, because it means the tenant gets the remainder of their deposit back much faster and you don't have to spend time putting together evidence for the adjudicator.

You can also see why it's so important to keep an emergency fund for each property: you might have planned to replace the carpet after ten years, but instead you need to find the £500 cost after two years with only £400 from the tenant to cover it.

Chapter 31

Eviction during a fixed term

We've already talked about how you can use a Section 21 notice to end a tenancy at (or after) the end of a fixed term. This is a "no fault" procedure: the term is ending (or has ended), you want the property back, no big deal.

If a tenant's bad behaviour means you want to get rid of them early, you'll need to use another tool: the Section 8 notice.

In this chapter we'll look at what it is, when you can use it, and what the major pitfalls are. Strap yourself in for this fantastically bumpy ride…

Using a Section 8 notice

Prepare to feel very grateful for the existence of the "no fault" Section 21 procedure you can use at the end of a fixed term, because the Section 8 process is slow, difficult, expensive and painful.

From the point of view of the court, you're attempting to throw someone out of their home during a period of time when you'd agreed that they could live there – so you'd better have a jolly good reason. This means that you'll definitely need to have a court hearing (unlike Section 21, when the judge will often just review the documents you submit without a hearing being needed), and judges are likely to find in the tenant's favour to avoid making them homeless if they possibly can.

For that reason, you should seek legal advice before issuing a Section 8 notice: I can only touch on the basics here, and any slight inaccuracy can result in the case being thrown out and having to start again.

Because a Section 8 is so drawn-out (and has no guarantee of success), it's often quicker to just wait and use a Section 21 notice – especially if the tenancy is somewhat near the end of its fixed term. As Section 21 is a "no fault" procedure, you can't claim for a reimbursement of any rent you're owed (as you can with Section 8), but you *can* use a Section 21 notice to get them out, then separately issue proceedings in the county court for the unpaid rent.

If you must serve a Section 8 notice, you'll need to use one (or more) of a number of pre-set "grounds" for doing so – which we'll take a look at now.

Grounds for eviction

There are 17 grounds for eviction you can use, of which eight are mandatory (the court *must* give you possession if they're proved) and nine are discretionary (the court can decide to give you possession or not based on the circumstances). You can state as many grounds as you want to if there are multiple reasons for wanting the tenants gone.

Ready for some grounds?

Let's start with the mandatory grounds – meaning that if you can prove at least one of these, the judge *must* grant possession:

- **Ground 1: landlord taking property as their own home.** Used when the landlord wants the property back to live in as their main home (or for their spouse or civil partner to do so).

- **Ground 2: mortgage property**. Used when a lender wants to repossess the property – so not much use for you.

- **Ground 3: holiday let.** Used when the tenancy is for a period of a maximum of eight months, and the property was occupied as a holiday let within the 12 months prior to the start of the tenancy. (If you want the option of using this ground, you'll need to give written notice that it may apply before the tenancy starts.)

- **Ground 4: property tied to an educational institution.** Used when the tenancy is for a period of no more than 12 months and the property belongs to an educational institution. I'd put money on your not being an educational institution, so that's not much use for you.

- **Ground 5: housing for a minister of religion.** Used when the property is being used by a minister of religion and is required for another minister. File under "niche".

- **Ground 6: refurbishment.** Used when the landlord wants to reconstruct, demolish or carry out works on part or all of the property, which cannot go ahead with the tenant there – perhaps because the tenant won't allow access. If this ground is used, the landlord has to pay reasonable removal costs.

- **Ground 7: death of the tenant.** Having the sole tenant die during a tenancy is (fortunately) very rare, and the implications of it are too complicated to get into here. In any case, you're very unlikely to ever use this ground.

- **Ground 7A: conviction for serious offence.** A new and relatively untested ground that was introduced in 2014, and is intended to make it possible to remove tenants who have been convicted of certain types of anti-social behaviour. As it's new and only applies to specific situations, this is currently a tricky one to use and expert legal advice would be needed

- **Ground 7B: service on landlord of notice by Secretary of State in respect of illegal immigrants.** Another new one, specifically to be used when you get notified by the Secretary of State that somebody living in the property doesn't have the Right To Rent. As you've done your checks (as described in Part 3), of course, this is unlikely to happen.

- **Ground 8: rent arrears**. To use this ground, at least two months' rent must be in arrears (assuming the rent is paid monthly). The two months of arrears must exist on the date that you serve the Section 8 notice, *and* on the date of the hearing. This is annoying, because the tenant can pay off some of the arrears just before the court date and therefore invalidate this ground.

And now, on to the discretionary grounds. As a rule, it's not worth starting the process using just the discretionary grounds, because courts are very unlikely to use their discretion to deprive someone of their home. Instead, you're more likely to get a result by waiting until one of the mandatory grounds applies – or even waiting until the end of the tenancy and serving a Section 21 instead. Nevertheless, here we go:

- **Ground 9: alternative accommodation.** This ground states that alternative accommodation will be available for the tenant in the case that the possession order is made, and that the landlord has to pay reasonable removal expenses. This isn't a reason in itself, but can be used to show that the *main* reason given won't leave the tenant homeless.

- **Ground 10: rent arrears.** Used when *any* amount of rent is due on the date that the Section 8 notice is served and is still due on the date that proceedings begin.

- **Ground 11: regular failure to pay rent.** Used when the tenant has failed on a regular basis to pay the rent.

- **Ground 12: breach of tenancy agreement.** Used when there has been a breach of any term of the tenancy agreement.

- **Ground 13: neglect of property.** Used when the property has been neglected by the tenant (or someone who the tenant has allowed to occupy the property), and as a result the condition of the property has deteriorated.

- **Ground 14: anti-social behaviour.** Used when the tenant has, in the precise wording of the Housing Act: "caused problems with neighbours, visitors or anyone else; has used the property for illegal or immoral purposes and received a conviction for this; or has received a conviction for an indictable offence in or near the property."

- **Ground 14a: domestic violence.** Used when the property is occupied by a couple and one person leaves due to violence or threats from the other. This ground only applies to property that is owned by a charitable housing trust or registered social landlord, so no use to you.

- **Ground 15: poor treatment of furnishings.** Used when the furniture in the property has been treated badly by the tenant or someone who the tenant allows to live there. Feels a bit insignificant coming straight after "domestic violence", doesn't it?

- **Ground 16: tied to employment.** Used when the tenant was employed by the landlord of the property and has now left the landlord's employment.

- **Ground 17: false statements.** Used when the landlord was induced to grant the tenancy by a false statement made "knowingly or recklessly by the tenant, or a person acting at the tenant's instigation".

To help understand the process a little better, let's look at the typical grounds used to evict a tenant due to non-payment of rent – which is by far the most common reason for wanting to get someone out.

In theory, as soon as the tenant is in any kind of arrears, you can use Ground 10 ("Any amount of rent is in arrears at the date of service of the notice and remains unpaid on the date on which the proceedings for possession are begun") and/or Ground 11 ("The tenant has repeatedly failed to pay rent") to start eviction proceedings. But these are *discretionary* grounds, so as I said earlier, it would be unwise to rely on these alone: the court is very unlikely to choose to give you possession.

The *mandatory* ground relating to non-payment of rent is Ground 8: "At the date of service of the notice and at the date of the hearing, the tenant has not paid the rent... rent is payable monthly and at least two months' rent is unpaid".

So really, you need to wait until the tenant is two months in arrears before you serve a Section 8 notice using Ground 8. Assuming the tenant pays rent monthly in advance (as is usually the case), they become one month in arrears as soon as the rent is one day late – so they're effectively two months in arrears after one month and one day of non-payment, and the Section 8 notice can be served.

The fly in the ointment is that if the tenant pays off some of the arrears before the court hearing, Ground 8 can no longer be proved and possession won't be granted. For that reason it's common to also chuck in Ground 10 and Ground 11 – which, while discretionary, might help the judge to find in your favour.

How to serve a Section 8 notice

You can download a Section 8 notice from the gov.uk website (search "assured tenancy forms", and you want Form 3), but again: if you make any mistakes, the whole thing will be thrown out and you'll have to start again, so it's advisable to get legal help rather than attempt a bit of DIY.

At Yellow Lettings we use a specialist company to help us with evictions. Register this book at www.propertygeek.net/landlord and I'll send you their details.

The notice needs to have an expiry date after which court proceedings can begin – which has the effect of saying to the tenant, "Look, you have this many days to rectify the problem or I'll see you in court." For the grounds relating to non-payment of rent, this should be at least 14 days from the date the notice is served (the notice period is longer for some other less-common grounds, so do check if you plan to use any of them).

The process for calculating when the notice is deemed to be "served" is the same as we talked about earlier with Section 21 notices (so I won't repeat it here), and it's worth adding on a few extra days – just in case the notice is served late for any reason.

Tenants will sometimes leave once they receive the Section 8 notice, because they want to avoid court proceedings. It means you'll have to try to get a county court judgment (CCJ) to claim the unpaid rent from them, but at least you'll be able to re-let the property.

If the 14 days expire and they haven't left *or* remedied the situation, you'll need to apply to your local court for a hearing – and if all goes well at the hearing, a possession order will be granted. If the possession order doesn't have the desired effect, you can (just like with the Section 21) go back to the court and get the bailiffs to evict. Also just like Section 21, you'll have to pay the court fees – and the bailiff fees if matters get that far.

On paper, none of this looks very scary, but there are any number of things that can frustrate a Section 8 procedure. A common one is the tenant paying just enough rent that the mandatory arrears ground doesn't apply at the time of the hearing, so only the discretionary grounds can be used – at which point a judge will very seldom grant possession. Just getting to court in the first place can take months by the time you've waited for a date

– so to get that far then *still* not get possession is nightmarish, because you'll now have even more arrears and be no further forward.

Again, don't panic!

This chapter on eviction is short, but that's not because it's a small topic: it could be (and probably is) the subject of an entire book.

The reason it's short is that it's *relatively* unlikely to ever concern you if you select tenants wisely, and I don't want to spend thousands of words boring and confusing you with details about a process you'll probably never need to go through. There are of course certain tenant groups who present a higher risk of not paying, but I wouldn't recommend you target this group unless you're confident in your ability to deal with everything that goes along with it.

Instead of fretting about worst-case scenarios, spend your mental energy doing these two things instead:

1. Thoroughly reference your tenants so you're less likely to get a bad one.

2. Do everything 100% by the book before and during the tenancy, so you know you can always rely on the Section 21 procedure to get rid of them eventually.

As I said above, although the eviction procedure can be complicated, drawn-out and nasty, tenants will often leave as soon as you serve the notice and they realise that you're really not messing around anymore. If you're unlucky enough to have non-paying tenants *and* they won't budge, I'd recommend using the services of an eviction specialist to ensure you don't make any mistakes that lengthen the process even further.

CONCLUSION

… And relax!

If you've read this book through from cover to cover, I salute you: there were some tough moments (calculating wear and tear comes to mind), but we got through it together.

Now, you're armed with everything you need to know to be a successful, relaxed and legally compliant landlord. You can feel smug that you're better informed than 95% of your peers, and your future tenants should feel lucky that their landlord is so committed to doing things properly.

While you can never be totally sure, following all the steps in this book should leave you in the best possible position – one where you won't get fined for doing something wrong, or have to deal with a tenant who trashes the place, or need to drag someone through the courts to get possession of your property back. As a result, you'll never know just how much more pleasant you've made your life by avoiding these nightmare scenarios, but trust me: I've seen them all, and making the effort to do things right is *far* less painful than having a tenancy go wrong.

I hope you enjoyed the book (at least in places) and are feeling confident about your role as a landlord. Now, make sure you keep that knowledge up-to-date: **just register your copy of the book at www.propertygeek.net/landlord and I'll email you whenever there's an important change you need to know about.**

If you're interested in hiring a letting agent, basic tax and accounting, or learning about letting HMOs or properties in Scotland, read on for the bonus chapters. Otherwise, I'll leave you here – thank you for reading, and good luck!

OTHER BOOKS BY ROB DIX

THE COMPLETE GUIDE TO PROPERTY INVESTMENT

Over the last 20 years, more than a million Brits have made life-changing profits from buy-to-let. But as prices keep rising and the tax landscape changes, investors need to get smarter in order to succeed.

It's far from "game over", but the game is changing… for the better. The unwary and under-prepared will be squeezed from the market – leaving educated, strategic investors to have their best decade yet.

The Complete Guide To Property Investment gives you the insight, information and action plan you need to navigate this new property landscape and come out on top.

It starts by demonstrating – with real-life examples – a range of strategies suited to achieving different investment goals. Then it takes you step by step through every aspect of researching, financing, buying and managing investment properties.

Get it on paperback, Kindle and audiobook: search "Rob Dix" on Amazon.

PROPERTY INVESTMENT FOR BEGINNERS

Despite some ups and downs along the way, property has been one of the best investments of the last 20 years – and you're convinced it could be your key to financial freedom. And it could. But where do you start?

Do you invest near where you live, or wherever yields are best? Do you rent to families, or professionals, or students? Should you be trawling through Rightmove or lurking at property auctions?

This short book covers the big questions you should be asking yourself before you so much as glance at an estate agent's window. It contains a **jargon-free explanation** of basic investment principles, summaries of the major post-crunch investment strategies, and advice on developing a mindset that will support your long-term success.

Get it on paperback, Kindle and audiobook: search "Rob Dix" on Amazon.

BEYOND THE BRICKS

What does it take to be successful in property investment? How can you start with nothing but a very ordinary level of savings, and amass a portfolio that means you'll never need to work for anyone else again?

Beyond The Bricks is a window into the lives of 9 UK-based investors who've done exactly that. Through long-form interviews with them, we learn exactly how they did it, what their lives are like now, and what they recommend to anyone just starting out.

Of course, "success" is a relative term. During the book you'll meet people ranging from Mark, who amassed a portfolio worth millions, to Serena, whose few houses saved her family from financial ruin. And along the way you'll meet Kim, who was unstoppable prior to the credit crunch, nearly lost everything, and found an innovative way to stay afloat.

The day-to-day life of a property investor isn't necessarily what you'd expect either. Fast cars and exotic holidays are represented... but so too are sprinting in pursuit of rent cheques, pottering around in a dressing gown all day, and helping a tenant with cancer by driving her to hospital appointments.

This book is less of a "how to" than a "how you could". It won't give you one formula for success, but many practical ideas and inspiring examples that you can use to craft your own property investment story.

With all jargon clearly explained, this book will be an educational and entertaining read for those who are yet to get started, as well as a rich source of new ideas for more experienced investors.

Get it on paperback, Kindle and audiobook: search "Rob Dix" on Amazon.

BONUS 1:
WORKING WITH A LETTING AGENT

"Bloody hell!" you might be thinking. "There's no way I've got time to bother dealing with everything in this book! I work hard all week, and I've got better things to do with my Sundays than exchange emails about mould and argue about how many years a carpet should last for."

If that's *exactly* what you're thinking, fair enough: managing a property most certainly isn't for everyone. If you don't have the time, or you don't live nearby, or you've just got things you'd rather be doing, that's totally fine – and that's why letting agencies exist.

So in this section, I'll tell you a little bit more about how letting agents work. Then I'll help you to not only find a good one, but also develop a good working relationship with them.

Types of agency service

Before making the final decision on whether to use a letting agent, it's helpful to understand the two main types of service on offer and what they include.

Let Only service

This is where the letting agent markets the property, finds a tenant, and goes through the process as far as checking them in and registering the deposit – pretty much everything in Parts 2 and 3 of this book, in fact. As soon as the tenant is in, you're on your own.

Fees for a Let Only service are sometimes charged as a percentage of the annual rent (something in the range of 5–8% is probably typical), and sometimes as a one-off fee (maybe £200–£500). Either way, the fee is normally taken in full from the first month's rent. If your agency goes down the percentage route and the tenancy doesn't last as long as planned (for example, the tenancy is for a year but the tenant exercises a break clause after six months), you'll be refunded the portion that relates to the part of the tenancy that didn't end up happening.

In addition to the Let Only fee, you'll be required to pay for any certificates that are needed – like an EPC, gas safety certificate and so on. The agent can arrange these using their own contractors, or you can arrange your own. Some agents will charge you extra for the inventory, whereas others won't – so do check.

Fully managed service

Full management includes (or should include) everything from Part 2 of the book onwards. While the agent will need your input on some decisions, they will be the first point of contact for any issues and should take the lead on every aspect of letting and managing the property .

The key aspects of a management service are:

- Collecting and passing on the rent, and chasing it up if it isn't paid on time

- Inspecting the property regularly, and updating you on its condition

- Arranging any maintenance that is needed

- Taking care of your legal obligations, such as gas safety certificates

- Responding promptly to tenant requests and keeping them happy

- Handling rent increases, renewals, check-outs and so on (the degree of assistance they give you with evictions will be covered in their terms of business)

Fees for management are usually charged as a percentage of the rent, often in the range of anything from 7% to 15%. There may also be a letting fee to cover the cost of finding the tenants in the first place – or this might be absorbed into the management fee.

The fee should always be for a percentage of the rent *collected* rather than the rent *due*, which isn't the same thing: you don't want your agent to be billing you a management fee when the rent isn't being paid for whatever reason, as it's their responsibility to sort it out – so read the small print.

The key trait to look for in any agent (but especially for full management) is *proactivity*. You shouldn't have to ask if they've done things: they should be telling you about things they've already done. If there's an issue, they should be coming to you with a proposed solution rather than calling you and saying "The boiler's broken – what should we do?" Because, frankly, if your agent is just relaying on what your tenant says, you might as well just deal with the tenant directly and save yourself some money.

Should you use a letting agent?

A *good* agent offers fantastic value for money. A *not-so-good* letting agent certainly doesn't – and in fact they can make your life even harder than if you were doing it all yourself. I'll show you how to detect and avoid those kinds of agent later.

The decision about whether to use a letting agent really comes down to the value you place on your time, how you enjoy spending that time, and how confident you feel in your ability to manage a property yourself.

Valuing your time

Let's say you use an agent to perform a Let Only service (which, as mentioned, encompasses pretty much everything in Part 2), and they charge you £250. If you value your time at £100 per hour, then it's a good deal for you if the process would take you longer than 2.5 hours. Given all the correspondence, viewings, referencing and paperwork that it involves, I think it almost certainly would take longer than that – even if you've got your systems down to a really fine art.

The same logic applies to full management too. By way of example, let's say your property commands a monthly rent of £500, and you're paying a pretty typical management fee of 10% – so £50 per month. If you value your time at £100 per hour, then it's a good deal for you if managing your property would take more than 30 minutes per month. Some months it would probably take two minutes to check your bank balance and that's it, but in a month where there's an issue and you have to start ringing around for tradespeople, it could easy take several hours.

The concept of assigning a monetary figure to your time isn't something that people typically do, but you should – given that it's the only truly finite resource you have. If you have a job, it's easy to do: take your annual net salary, and divide it by 1750 (the number of working hours in a year, based on a 35-hour week) to arrive at your hourly rate.

It's an important measure that can put a whole new spin on

whether it's better to spend an hour washing the car yourself to save paying £4 to have it done at a car wash. But it's not strictly accurate, because as a typical employee you generally can't choose to work one more hour and earn one more hour's pay. What you're doing more usually is giving up your leisure time, which is why it's important to consider what you enjoy too.

Considering what you enjoy

Some people love the business of being a landlord. I know plenty of people who get a huge kick out of interviewing potential tenants, keeping them happy, and leaping into action whenever there's something that needs fixing. For these people, using a letting agent would be a terrible idea: it would deprive them of something they enjoy, and they'd be paying for the privilege.

My partner at Yellow Lettings, Rob Bence, is the exact opposite: he's perfectly capable of talking to tenants and dealing with admin, but he doesn't enjoy it and he prefers to spend his time focusing on what he's best at. If there were only one letting agent left on earth and they charged 50% of the rent, he'd probably still use them.

I fall somewhere in the middle. I actually quite enjoy being hands-on, but I have a very busy working life – and in my limited leisure time, there are things I enjoy doing more than managing properties.

Ultimately, most of us are investing in property now so that we can enjoy a better lifestyle in the future, but let's not forget about that lifestyle now: if you enjoy being a landlord, don't let anyone stop you, but there's no sense in being a martyr just to save a few quid.

Confidence

The final factor is confidence: how much do you back yourself to successfully complete all the tasks that go along with being a landlord? The consequences for getting it wrong can be severe – legally as well as financially, as there's a mountain of legislation to comply with, and it's changing all the time.

This is where enjoyment comes back into the picture, because you're more likely to keep on top of best practices and changes in the law if it's something you enjoy doing. But that aside, managing a property involves a broad range of skills, so you need to judge how confident you are that you can make a good job of it.

It doesn't take much of a knowledge gap to leave you exposed. For example, if you fail to correctly register a deposit, you could be sued for up to three times its value. Or you might end up overpaying for a repair because you don't have the contacts or the knowledge of how much it should cost you.

It's natural for your confidence to start out low then increase with experience, so you might want to use a letting agent for your first property, keep an eye on what they're doing while referring back to this book, then decide to take on the job yourself when the tenants move out. Conversely, some people are highly confident and prefer to jump right in at the start, do everything themselves to figure out how it all works, then pass it over to a letting agent after a year or two when they're in a better position to judge whether they're doing their job properly.

And the decision is...

There's no doubt that using a letting agent is the right choice for a lot of people – otherwise there wouldn't be so many of us in business. But then there are also a huge number of landlords who happily self-manage, so it's really a case of knowing yourself and taking account of the money, what you enjoy, and how confident you feel. And remember: once you've started going down one route, it doesn't mean you're tied into it forever.

However, what you *really* don't want to do is decide to use an agent and then realise that they don't have a clue what they're doing – meaning they could land you in hot legal water, and you're spending all your time running around after the agent instead of the tenant.

That's why finding a good agent is paramount – and handily, it's the topic of the next section.

Finding a good agent

It probably hasn't escaped your attention that letting agents are about as popular as... actually, I can't even think of a suitable simile because letting agents are less popular than anything else in the modern world.

There's a reason for this. Letting agency is a sector with no mandatory regulation, so anyone can set up shop and start collecting fees without any kind of experience, knowledge, scruples or human emotions – and they frequently do. This makes it exceptionally important to do your due diligence when you're choosing who to work with.

(From 2018, letting agents in Scotland will need to join a register and show that they hold a relevant qualification.)

The consequences of a poor agent

The consequences of a bad agent can be both financially and legally serious.

For example, I once let a property through an agent who told me that the tenant had found bedbugs in one of the beds – and reported that their local contractor said it would take eight treatments to remove the problem, for a total cost of £1,400.

This is insane for two reasons. Firstly, it typically takes no more than two treatments to remove bedbugs and a more reasonable price would be in the region of £150–£250. And secondly, unless the bedbugs were present at the start of the tenancy or the tenancy agreement specifically said something to the contrary, it's generally accepted that it's the tenant's responsibility to pay for the treatment as they brought them into the property in the first place. (At the point they were reported, the tenancy was six months old, so they clearly hadn't been there from the start.)

Had I not done my research, I would have been hit with a totally unnecessary £1,400 bill – which shows how expensive just one issue can be when you're dealing with an inexperienced agent.

The legal consequences can be even more severe. Although an agent will normally take care of everything in Parts 2–5 if they're fully managing the property, it's imperative to remember that the legal responsibility ultimately falls on you. If the worst happens and a tenant is killed by a dodgy boiler, for example – and your agent had failed to arrange a valid gas safety certificate – it's you who'll end up in court (and maybe prison), and the defence that "my agent was meant to be doing it" won't get you anywhere at all.

That's why it's so important, even if you use an agent, to have a basic understanding of the topics we've covered in this book.

How to find a good agent

Short of a recommendation from someone you trust (which is always best), here's the process I recommend you follow when scouting out potential agents:

1.   Look on Rightmove to see which agencies seem to be marketing the most properties similar to yours in the immediate area. In many parts of the country, you'll find that one or two agencies specialise in properties at the low end of the market, and a couple more dominate the more expensive end of the market – and there are even

niches like Polish-run agencies that dominate areas where lots of Polish people choose to live.

2. Call anyone who's still in the running and get a feel for how you're treated on the phone. Personally, I'd like the agent to engage in a bit of a chat and share some thoughts on the local market rather than immediately try to take my phone number and commit to a "free market appraisal" (or similar, which is code for an invitation to come round and pitch to you in person).

3. Check whether the agents are members of a redress scheme – which means a body you can appeal to if the agent mistreats you. Since October 2014 it's been mandatory for agents to belong to a government-approved redress scheme: either The Property Ombudsman, Ombudsman Services Property or the Property Redress Scheme. If they don't, that's a major red flag because they're (deliberately or through negligence) not keeping up with current legislation. Just imagine everything else they're not doing!

4. Check whether they voluntarily belong to a trade body like ARLA or NALS. These bodies require their members to have client money protection (meaning that any funds they hold on your behalf, like the rent before passing it over, are insured) and abide by a certain code of practice, which can give you some degree of reassurance.

5. Use your gut feel and the knowledge you gain from this

book to decide if they seem to be proactive in their marketing and by-the-book in their procedures.

This is purely my own bias, but I'd always prefer an independent agent over a national chain – provided that they seem like a professional outfit based on the checks above and the questions in the next section. That's because staff at the chains tend to hop from company to company down the high street, so there's very little continuity. Established local agencies, on the other hand, are more likely to have staff who've been there for years and are totally on top of their job. I also prefer a standalone letting agency to one that does both sales and lettings, simply because it's what they specialise in. At agencies that do both, lettings can be an afterthought.

There are plenty of exceptions, of course, but those are rules of thumb that have generally worked for me.

Interviewing a potential agent

Having run these basic checks, I'd recommend asking some specific questions:

- Who will be my point of contact? How long have they been with the company?

- Can I see a copy of your terms of business?

- Other than your Let Only fee / management fees, what other fees should I be aware of?

- Do you charge me or my tenant for renewing the tenancy?

- Do you mark up maintenance quotes or charge a fee for arranging maintenance?

- Which tenancy deposit protection scheme do you use?

- Do you have client money protection?

- Is there a number tenants can call if they have an out-of-hours emergency?

It's up to you what you regard as acceptable answers (although personally, I wouldn't consider working with an agent who tried to clobber me with *any* extra fees for maintenance, renewals or anything else they can dream up), but you should be able to get an idea of whether the person you're speaking to is confident or just bluffing their way through. You'll never *really* know until you start, but comprehensive research plus targeted questions plus gut feel should get you a long way.

Working with your agent

As both a landlord and the owner of a letting agency, I feel well qualified to tell you that, frankly, landlords can be a right pain in the neck sometimes. But they can also be brilliant – and the key characteristic of the brilliant landlords is that they strike a balance between being responsive and letting us get on with it.

Responsiveness is absolutely critical. Appointing an agent

doesn't mean you can just wash your hands of the whole thing, turn off your phone and check back in a few years: while the agent is on the front line for anything that comes up, they'll sometimes need your input – and when they do, they'll need it *quickly*.

The nightmare situation as an agent is receiving a tenant's complaint about an issue, doing all the running around to get quotes and find the best solution, then being totally unable to pin down the landlord to get the go-ahead to take action. In the meantime, the agent is getting an earful on a daily basis from a frustrated tenant, and the issue itself could be getting worse through inaction – which means the landlord will be unhappy when they finally surface.

But then, the opposite extreme – "keeping a dog and barking yourself" – isn't a lot of fun either. There are landlords who are constantly checking up, asking if things have been done, and even communicating with the tenant directly – and if they want to be that hands-on, they would really be better off not having an agent at all.

It's not an easy balance to strike, but once you're there it makes for a much happier relationship all round. My recommendation is to start by erring on the side of checking up (because you never know if a new agent is doing their job properly), then easing off over time. But however much you ease off, always get back to your agent within 48 hours if they have a query.

How to fire your agent

What if, despite doing everything in your power to select the right agent and form a good working relationship with them, they still do a shoddy job?

Unfortunately, it does happen: a change of personnel or a sudden growth spurt, and your previously reliable agent starts letting things slip. If it *does* happen, the action you can take will be governed by the agreement you signed with the agent in the first place.

Typically, the agreement will say that you have to stick with the agent until the tenant that they found moves out. If you want to leave early, you'll have to pay the fees they would have received up until the end of the tenancy – and perhaps an extra termination fee.

This leaves you with three choices: wait until the tenant moves out and then leave, leave early and pay, or leave early *without* paying and take the calculated risk that they won't take you to court for such a small amount of money.

Where at all possible, I'd recommend just sticking with it until the tenant leaves. Not only is it what you agreed to in the first place, but the process of switching isn't straightforward: you'll need to re-protect the tenant's deposit (which will involve returning it to the tenant then getting it back from them, if it's in an insurance rather than custodial scheme), get them to change their standing order, and (if you want to take out Rent Guarantee Insurance) put them through referencing again.

Of course, if the agent is doing a truly shocking job and putting your property at risk, you might have no choice but to get out early. Write to them requesting early release from your agreement on the grounds that they haven't performed the duties they were supposed to (make sure you keep detailed notes of their failings), and hopefully they'll let you go. If not, you could unilaterally withdraw and hope they won't like the idea of a court case where their failings will be exposed and they'll only stand to recoup a few hundred pounds in fees.

BONUS 2:
BASIC PROPERTY TAX AND ACCOUNTING

If you have income from property, you'll need to pay tax on it. That unfortunate reality dominates the thoughts of a lot of property investors – especially given developments in recent years, which we'll cover in a moment.

I've included this chapter about tax and accounting as a bonus because it's not directly related to how to be a landlord, but I thought it was important to flag up roughly what your obligations are and what you might want to be thinking further about. The information is abridged and adapted from Chapter 13 of my book The Complete Guide To Property Investment (www.propertygeek.net/completeguide).

Do bear in mind, though, that I'm far from being an accountant and I'm not qualified to give financial advice. Anything to do with tax comes in many shades of grey (and not even the fun ones), so my only intention here is to explain the very basics and get you thinking about how tax might apply to your own situation. Before taking any action, you should read much more widely and take professional advice.

The basics

Once you've bought a property in your own name, it's your responsibility to tell HMRC that they now have another method by which they can gouge money out of you. They've got no way of automatically knowing, which is great until they catch up with you a few years later and take action against you for tax evasion.

If you already fill in a tax return, all you need to do is complete an extra page for your new property income. But if you're currently taxed via your employer, you need to notify HMRC of your need to complete a tax return. The easiest way is to call them using the details on their website.

Filling in that tax return used to be pretty straightforward: take the rental income, deduct all the allowable costs you incurred (which we'll come to), and whatever's left over is your profit. That profit is split between any joint owners, and it's added to your other sources of income when calculating the tax you owe.

I say "used" to be straightforward because of changes to the treatment of mortgage interest, which took effect from April 2017. For the next few years, it's going to be much more complicated to work out your tax position – and I'll discuss this more in the next section.

Alternatively, if you buy a property within a company rather than in your own name, that company will need to file accounts. Then, when you draw profits out of the company, you'll be in exactly the same position as above: you'll either declare that income on your tax return if you already complete one, or let HMRC know that you now need to.

In terms of record keeping, everything becomes a lot easier if you have a separate bank account that's used solely for property transactions. Any normal current account will do: just have the rent as the only payment coming in, and expenses going out as direct debits or charged to the associated debit card. If you have a linked savings account, you can also get in the habit of regularly transferring funds across to cover tax and/or serve as a contingency fund. Whether you do the bookkeeping yourself or let your accountant handle it, it's a lot easier when the transactions are separated rather than intermingled with your own finances.

Speaking of which, do you need an accountant? When you're just starting out, not necessarily: if the sums are small, it's unlikely that an accountant will be able to save you more than they're costing you (as long as you get yourself clued up about what you can claim). But if you're lacking in confidence or time, there's no reason not to get help.

If you do choose to get help from an accountant, it's best if you use a property specialist. I use the accountant who does the books for my business because I consider myself to be on top of the property side of things, but if I weren't so involved I'd definitely want to have a specialist on my team.

Mortgage interest

The chancellor of the exchequer isn't going to win many popularity contests at the best of times, but in the summer of 2015 George Osborne announced a change that prompted a spike in Amazon sales of voodoo dolls (I imagine) among property investors.

Before getting into the details, it's important to be clear that this only affects *individual* property investors: the treatment of property within companies is the same as it was before.

So what is this change, and why is it so universally loathed and protested against? It all revolves around how mortgage interest payments are treated in your property accounts.

Previously, property investment income would be treated in the same way as any other business: rent comes in, expenses go out, profit is what remains – and that profit is taxed. If you take out a mortgage to acquire a buy-to-let property, the monthly interest payments are considered to be a cost of doing business – and therefore they're deducted along with all your other costs before calculating the profit that's left over.

To put that into numbers:

- £10,000 rental income

- £5,000 mortgage interest costs

- £1,000 other costs

- = £4,000 profit

That £4,000 profit would be subject to your normal rate of tax – currently 20% for a basic rate taxpayer (meaning a tax bill of £800) and 40% for a higher rate taxpayer (meaning a tax bill of £1,600).

Here's the change: from April 2017, *mortgage interest can no longer be deducted as a cost of doing business*. Instead of deducting it before arriving at your profit figure, you first calculate your profit and then claim a *basic rate allowance* (currently 20%) for your mortgage interest before calculating the tax due.

This becomes a lot clearer with the help of an example:

- £10,000 rental income

- [£5,000 mortgage interest costs – NOT DEDUCTED]

- £1,000 other costs

- = £9,000 profit

- Allowance to apply: 20% of £5,000 interest costs = £1,000

A 20% taxpayer would therefore owe £1,800 in tax on their

profit (20% of £9,000), then claim the allowance of £1,000, leaving them with a final tax bill of £800. A 40% taxpayer would owe £3,600 in tax on their profit (40% of £9,000), then claim the allowance of £1,000, leaving them with a final tax bill of £2,600.

Two things happen as a result of this change.

The basic rate taxpayer appears to end up paying the same amount, so let's first take the case of a higher rate taxpayer. Clearly they have a higher tax bill, which was exactly the point of this new method. The intention is to "level the playing field" between owner-occupiers who can't offset their interest against tax and property investors who can, but to limit that effect to higher rate taxpayers (who I presume they think can afford it).

Investors were furious about the principle of the change, because the financing costs associated with acquiring capital assets are an allowable expense for every other type of business. (And because this new method doesn't apply to properties owned within a company, it's also an allowable expense for participants in the *same* industry if they have a different corporate structure.) But worse than the principle is the reality that if a higher rate taxpayer is highly leveraged, they can end up paying more in tax than they make in profit.

For example:

- A property worth £200,000 with a mortgage of 80% of its value (£160,000) at an interest rate of 5%

- £12,000 rental income

- [£8,000 mortgage interest costs - NOT DEDUCTED]

- £1,500 other costs

- = £10,500 profit

- Allowance to apply: 20% of £8,000 interest costs = £1,600

So the amount of actual cash that the investor has in their pocket after paying all their expenses is £2,500 (£12,000 - £8,000 - £1,500). Previously this would have resulted in a tax bill of £1,000 (40% of £2,500) and a post-tax profit of £1,500.

But their tax bill is now calculated as 40% of £10,500 (£4,200), minus the £1,600 allowance. That leaves them with a tax bill of £2,600 – which means they're now making a £100 loss!

Bad news, then, for higher rate taxpayers. But did you catch the second thing that happened? Because profit is now calculated *before* interest is deducted or allowances are claimed, *everyone's* income now appears to be higher. That means that a lot of investors who were previously basic rate taxpayers are being pulled into the higher bracket – even if their portfolio is barely profitable.

To complicate matters further, the new method started being phased in gradually from April 2017 and doesn't come into effect fully until April 2020. From April 2017 the new method applies to 25% of your interest cost (and you can deduct the rest as before), then it's 50% from April 2018, and 75% from April 2019 before it reaches 100% in April 2020.

Chances are, you're now asking yourself a very good question: if the new method is worse and it only applies to individual investors, is it better to buy properties within the structure of a company?

Should you incorporate?

You can buy a property either as an individual (or couple), or by forming a company and having that company be the owner of the property.

There are two big advantages to investing through a company:

- You swerve the new treatment of mortgage interest, allowing you to deduct it in full before calculating your profit. (Although, note of caution: *for now*. If enough investors flee to companies, there's nothing to stop the government dreaming up a new tax that will nullify the benefit.)

- Your profits are subject to corporation tax rather than income tax, which will make a significant difference if you're a higher rate taxpayer – because corporation tax is currently 20%, compared to the higher rates of income tax which are 40% and 45%.

If you already own a property and you want these tax advantages, you'll need to sell your property (at its true market price) from yourself to your company – which throws up complications in terms of stamp duty, capital gains tax (CGT) and needing to switch mortgages. Take advice from an accountant if this is something you think you might want to do.

For properties you buy in the future, there's no such complication: you could buy them as a company and get yourself those tax benefits. But there are drawbacks too:

- If you want to draw profits out of the company to spend, you'll do so in the form of dividends and be taxed for doing so – meaning that you could end up no further ahead than if you'd just bought in your own name and paid income tax.

  For example, a £1,000 profit taxed at an income tax rate of 40% leaves you with £600. A £1,000 profit taxed at a corporation tax rate of 20% leaves you with £800 – but you then pay a dividend tax rate of 32.5% if you're a higher rate taxpayer (after the first £2,000 of dividends, which are tax-free) when you want to access the £800, leaving you with £540. So in this scenario, assuming you've already used up your dividend allowance, you end up worse off than you would have been by just paying income tax in the first place.

- If you've been renting out a property for a while and then choose to sell it, as an individual you can use your annual CGT allowance so you're not taxed on the full amount of the gain. A company doesn't have a CGT allowance, so would end up paying more tax than an individual when selling the property.

Another disadvantage – although one that is improving rapidly – is that the number of lenders willing to lend to companies is more limited than it is for individuals. This tends to mean higher interest rates, lower loan-to-value ratios and higher arrangement fees. Even so, you might end up with a mortgage that's a bit more expensive but end up saving a lot of tax as a result – so you need to run your own personal numbers.

Because dramatically more investors have started using corporate vehicles over the last year or two, lenders have responded accordingly and introduced more products with improved rates. This is only going to continue – so a good mortgage adviser to guide you through the options will be, as always, your best friend.

So should you incorporate? As a very general rule of thumb (which definitely doesn't constitute tax advice), investors tend to find it advantageous to buy within a company if they plan to leave the profits to build up within the company for future purchases until (for example) they quit full-time work and their income falls, meaning they'll only be paying basic rate tax and the dividends they take from the company will be taxed at 7.5% rather than 32.5%. If they plan to withdraw the profits as personal income now, it's far more of a toss-up and it could well be better *not* to incorporate.

Again, I remind you that this is nothing more than a brief summary from a non-expert. Weighing up the pros and cons and applying them to your own present situation and long-term goals is no easy matter – and the right decision will depend on your current earnings, what you plan to do with the profits, what the future tax position of your portfolio is likely to be, whether you'll be selling properties, how much leverage you use, and many, many other factors. In short, it's something you should take professional advice about rather than rely solely on a book.

Allowable expenses

In the course of letting a property you'll incur expenses, and many of those expenses can be deducted from your income before arriving at your profit. The name of the game, then, is to make sure you claim every expense that you legitimately can: if you're paying tax on your profits at a rate of 40%, remembering to claim an extra £100 in expenses will reduce your tax bill by £40. Clearly it makes no sense to incur expenses for the sake of it, but you should get the most out of the expenses you can't avoid… and even be a bit strategic about it to extract maximum benefit.

Expenses fall into two different categories: *capital* expenditure, and *revenue* expenditure.

Capital expenditure relates to the costs of acquiring assets (in our case, that means properties), and costs relating to anything you do with that asset to materially increase its value. Examples would include:

- The actual purchase price of the property

- Your legal fees for arranging the purchase

- Any refurbishment work you do to a property *before letting it out for the first time* (this becomes important in the next section)

- Any work you do to the property that improves it (and thus could increase its value), such as converting the loft or adding an en suite bathroom

Capital expenditure can't be deducted from your profits in the year in which you incur the expense. Instead, you can only reclaim these costs when you eventually *sell* the property.

For example, if you buy a property for £100,000, pay £2,000 in legal fees and immediately spend £50,000 refurbishing it, that's £152,000 in capital expenditure. If you sell the property for £300,000 in the future, you can deduct that £152,000 before calculating the CGT you will owe.

Expenses categorised as "capital" are no fun. You're shelling out now and getting nothing back for potentially decades – and by the time you can reclaim them, inflation means that the relief you're getting will be worth less to you than you paid out in the first place.

Everything that doesn't fall under the category of capital expenditure is automatically revenue expenditure instead. Revenue expenditure is much more like it: you incur a cost today, and can immediately offset it against your income. Examples include:

- Any fees you're charged by a letting agent

- Any bills you pay as part of the rent

- Any repairs you need to make to the property

- Any furniture you buy for the property

- Any refurbishment you do *after* the property has already been let out, which broadly just *restores it to its previous condition* rather than makes an improvement (for example, redecorating, or replacing a dated bathroom suite with a new one that looks more modern but isn't "better" in terms of its facilities)

In addition to these pretty obvious revenue expenses relating to specific properties, there's a range of more general expenses that also fall under the "revenue" category:

- Any relevant costs you incur for *seven years* prior to your property business starting – which could be tax advice, travel, business cards or anything else you can think of. Unfortunately, however, you can't make any claims relating to aborted transactions – so if you got a survey done on a property that subsequently fell through, that's not allowable

- Any mileage you use in the course of property activities, which can be claimed at standard HMRC business rates

- The costs of education, as long as it's classed as improving an existing skill rather than acquiring a new one

- Sustenance costs while running your business, within reason – so keep your receipts for the odd sandwich and coffee while you're out and about on property-related business

- Postage costs, such as sending documents to solicitors

- Telephone costs

- An allowance for using your home as an office (which you can claim if you run your business from home)

And more. As with everything in tax, there are grey areas aplenty here – which is why it's worth paying an accountant at some point. If you're just starting out, no number of receipts for stamps and sandwiches will save you as much as an accountant charges, but when you get to a certain scale it can give you the confidence to claim expenses that you weren't sure about or possibly weren't even aware of.

Losses and tax planning

The wonderful thing about tax (now there's a phrase I never

thought I'd type) is that losses can be carried forward for as long as your business exists, until they're "wiped out" by equivalent profits.

To give an example, say you buy a property in Year 1 and in the process you pay your broker's fees and buy some white goods for the kitchen, then go on a full-day course (all classified as revenue expenses) – for a total spend of £3,000 before any rent comes in. That loss of £3,000 is carried forward to Year 2, during which you make a profit of £2,000. That means you still have an overall loss of £1,000 to carry forward to Year 3, which is the point at which you're first on track to become profitable and have tax to pay.

It's important to realise that profits and losses are calculated across your portfolio as a whole – so in any given year if you incur a whole load of costs on one particular property (as long as they're classified as "revenue" in nature), these costs will reduce or eliminate the profit you would otherwise have made on the rest of your portfolio. However, you can't offset property losses against *other* sources of income – your property portfolio is effectively a separate "business" in itself, even if you own the properties in your own name.

Once you appreciate these facts (that the profits/losses that determine tax liability are calculated across the whole portfolio, and losses can be carried forward), you start to see that while you're expanding your portfolio, it's possible to structure your affairs to pay less tax than you might think.

Let's see how. Say you buy a property that's fundamentally sound but somewhat dated internally, and it comes with a tenant already in situ. Six months later, the tenant gives notice and you take the opportunity to refurbish the property before you move the next tenant in – costing £7,000.

As we saw in the last section, if you'd conducted this refurbishment before letting the property out for the first time, it would have been categorised as "capital" in nature – whether that refurbishment had constituted "improvement" or not. But once the property has already been let by you for a period of time, anything that isn't an improvement can be classified as a "revenue" expense.

Let's say the refurbishment consisted of replacing single-glazed windows with double glazing (not considered an improvement, because putting in single glazing nowadays isn't an option), replacing a grotty old bathroom suite (an improvement aesthetically but not functionally, which is critical) and giving the whole place new carpets and a lick of paint. Those changes might allow you to increase the rent, and might even increase the value of the property if you ever wanted to refinance or sell it on – but nevertheless, they're "revenue" in nature.

That £7,000 spend might eliminate the profit from the rest of your portfolio, or even give you a loss to carry forward. So if you're in acquisition mode and buying one such property per year, you may not have tax to worry about for quite a while.

There are important subtleties in here. For a start, you'd need to make sure that your expenses were *genuinely* revenue in nature – and if the refurbishment included an element of capital improvement too, you should try to get any tradespeople to separate out their invoices to keep it neat. For example, if the same company added a loft conversion (improvement, hence capital) and repainted all the existing internal walls (reinstatement, hence revenue) you should ask them to issue a separate invoice for each job. Secondly, enough time needs to elapse for you not to be "gaming the system": there are no hard and fast rules, but if you bought a property, let it out for a month, refurbished it, let it for another few months and sold it, eyebrows might be raised at HMRC. Or they might not – such is the nature of grey areas – but the eyebrow raise might happen after you've done the same thing for the fourth time in two years.

In short, I'm saying that by understanding the basics of how property profits are taxed, you can optimise your activities to keep your tax bill down – especially while you're in the acquisition phase. You can see how, timed correctly, you could avoid making a paper profit for years – perhaps until your income from other sources (such as employment) has dropped off and put you into a lower tax bracket, for example.

But I'll say it one last time: *this is not a tax book.* I want to give you enough knowledge to get you thinking about what's possible, but please, make sure this is the start of your education process rather than the end. Take professional advice rather than rely on what you read in this book or online, and make sure you're not knowingly or unknowingly breaking any rules or storing up unintended consequences.

It may be tempting to stretch the rules and sail close to the wind, but it's not worth the stress. While an investigation is unlikely to happen, I prefer to make sure I could sit across the table from an HMRC representative and confidently explain my tax arrangements without any concern.

BONUS 3:
HMOs

Running an HMO – a "house in multiple occupation" – is, on paper, very similar to letting and managing any other property. But while the paperwork, principles and underlying laws are the same, the volume and variety of tasks involved in managing an HMO require a totally different mindset and approach.

In this bonus chapter I'll share some tips for letting and managing HMOs – but first we need to define what an HMO actually *is*, then understand the extra legalities that come along with this type of property.

What is an HMO?

The definition of an HMO is a home made up of *three or more people* who form *two or more households*.

So:

- Two unrelated individuals living in separate rooms of the same house would *not* create an HMO because there must be three or more people.

- Two couples living in separate rooms of the same house *would* be an HMO, because there are four individuals and two "households".

- Five unrelated individuals living in separate rooms would clearly be an HMO.

- One family of ten people – even if headed by an unmarried couple with step-children, foster children, aunts, grandparents and so on – would *not* be an HMO because they all form a single household together.

Earlier, I said that an HMO was a "home" rather than a "property". That's because if a property had been converted into completely self-contained flats, it wouldn't be an HMO even though a whole number of unrelated people live there. But *within* one of those flats, an HMO could be created if the occupiers meet the definition above.

Getting consent for an HMO

If you had a good time reading about the different situations in which licenses are and aren't required for regular properties, you'll lose your mind with excitement when we get into the details of HMO licensing. First, though, we need to take a quick detour via planning permission, which could affect your ability to set up an HMO in the first place.

Planning permission

In terms of planning law, a single-occupancy house has a different planning category (known as C3) from an HMO (known as C4) – even though the same building could be in single occupancy at one time and multiple occupancy at another.

In general, this isn't of any consequence. But each local authority has the ability to implement something called an *Article 4 directive* – meaning that you need to obtain planning permission to change a normal property into an HMO. They often choose to implement Article 4 in particular areas with high concentrations of HMOs, where they're worried about the consequences of having many multiple-occupancy households – such as areas with lots of students.

Because the point of Article 4 is to restrict the number of HMOs, councils are reluctant to grant planning permission in these areas. This means that if you want to let a property as an HMO, you need to either:

- Make sure Article 4 doesn't apply in that area

Or

- Buy a property that's already running as an HMO, because the planning status isn't affected by a change of owner

To check whether Article 4 applies, search for "[Name of local authority] Article 4" and see if anything comes up. If it is in force, you'll often find a map showing the affected area. If you're not sure, you can always call the local housing department.

Licenses

An HMO in England and Wales will *always* require a license if it meets the definition of a "large" HMO. This is known as "mandatory licensing".

(In Scotland, *all* HMOs require a mandatory license, whether they're large or not.)

To be a "large" HMO, the property must meet all three of these conditions:

- Five or more people live there

- They form two or more households

- The property is at least three storeys high

At the time of writing, a consultation is underway to remove the "three storeys high" requirement – which will pull more properties into requiring a mandatory license.

Local authorities can also decide to require that other HMOs (which don't meet the "large" definition) will also require a license. This is known as "additional licensing" – so check their website or call up to see if this applies.

Licenses are granted for up to five years, and always come with certain conditions:

- A gas safety certificate is obtained every year *and* supplied to the council

- An electrical safety inspection is carried out every five years

- Proper fire safety measures (including smoke detectors) are in place

- The property is free of serious hazards

- The property isn't overcrowded

- There are sufficient cooking, washing and rubbish disposal arrangements for the number of occupants

Local authorities have leeway in how they interpret these conditions – and they can be amazingly specific in their interpretation. For example, Bristol council requires that "Each toilet in a separate compartment is required to have a window equivalent to 1/20th of the floor area." Reading council requires two 13 amp electrical sockets per six people sharing a kitchen, "in addition to any serving major appliances, set at a convenient height and safe position".

Importantly, they can also set their own requirements about minimum acceptable bedroom sizes – so you might have a four-bedroom house that you want to turn into an HMO, but later find that only two of those bedrooms meet the council's minimum size requirements.

If you go to your local authority's website, you can normally download their full list of criteria – or if not, you can request to have it sent to you.

Before granting a license, a council official will inspect the property and bring their finest-tooth comb to assist them – so check the list a number of times that would put Santa to shame and make sure you've got a tick in every box. Also make a point of befriending the HMO officer: they'll be more likely to help you if they like you, and it will be useful to have them on your side for when something (inevitably) goes wrong later.

They won't just look at the property, by the way: when granting a license they'll also check that you're a "fit and proper person" to be managing it. Which you are, aren't you?

Given your undisputed fitness and properness, I know you wouldn't think, "Gosh this all sounds like a lot of hard work – but hey, councils are pretty inefficient so I just won't bother telling them and they probably won't notice." But just in case you were tempted…

- If you're convicted for running an HMO without a license when it should have one, you can be fined £20,000 plus costs (£50,000 in Scotland).

- You can also be ordered to repay up to a year's worth of rent to the occupants.

- *And* any Section 21 notice you serve to tenants won't be valid if you do it while the property doesn't have proper licensing arrangements.

So there you go.

Setting up an HMO

When you're setting up an HMO, you'll have all the same concerns as preparing any property to let: getting the right consents, meeting the safety requirements, refurbishing, and so on. You'll also need to make sure you meet all the requirements needed to be granted a license, if the property requires a mandatory license or additional licensing is in place.

With an HMO, your running costs will be higher than they are in a single let: you'll be responsible for paying the council tax, utility bills, and maybe even paying for a cleaner. This makes the *occupancy rate* very important: if you struggle to attract tenants for all the rooms most of the time, you'll still have the same overheads to pay and it'll be very difficult to make your numbers add up.

That means it's vital to get the specification of the refurbishment and quality of furnishing right at the start – so your rooms are competitive with the other options that are available locally.

Do some research (either by making friends with local landlords and asking to look around their rooms, or virtually checking out the competition on online lettings portals), and make sure you hit the mark when it comes to the expectations of your target market.

Finding HMO tenants

With HMOs, it's vital to have a solid process for finding tenants, because you're going to be almost permanently in recruitment mode: unlike a single let where you might just need to find a new tenant once per year or less, an HMO with six rooms will mean you're bound to have someone moving out every few months.

As mentioned all the way back in Part 2, Spareroom (www.spareroom.co.uk) is the most popular site for room rentals – although depending on your target market, you might also want to bring Gumtree (www.gumtree.com) into play, as well as the local paper and local universities.

Another invaluable source of HMO tenants is referrals from your existing occupants. A quick text or email to your current tenants – perhaps even with an incentive if they recommend someone who ends up taking the room – could save all manner of messing about with adverts. And although you (of course) won't scrimp on referencing, a referral from a *good* tenant is likely to have a better chance of working out than someone who's replied to an advert at random.

Once you've found somebody to take the room, the process for setting up the tenancy is exactly the same as for a single let: you'll still need to reference them (and establish their Right To

Rent), issue a tenancy agreement, conduct an inventory (just of the room, not the whole house), check them in, and protect their deposit.

As you'll be doing this more regularly than you would with a single let, it's even more important to find efficiencies. If you can incentivise existing tenants to conduct viewings so you don't have to, all the better – and there's all the more reason to set up payments by direct debit, and issue all the tenancy documents digitally.

Managing HMO tenants

While the process of *finding* tenants for an HMO isn't that different, *managing* those tenants is a totally different kettle of fish. Or possibly a kettle of something yucky that everyone's complaining about, or a kettle that you get called about at 6am because someone can't work out how to turn it on.

Yes, managing an HMO can be hard work, for lots of reasons:

- The facilities in the house are being used more intensively, so there will be more wear and tear to sort out.

- It's likely to be fully furnished (all the way down to cutlery and small appliances), so there's more to break or need replacing.

- Tenants who don't know each other may have conflicts

that need refereeing.

- There are multiple people who may be late in paying their rent and need chasing.

- There will often be someone "new" who doesn't know how things work and have questions to ask.

The more you can pre-empt, the better – so providing a house manual is more important than ever. At most times there will be a relative newcomer who doesn't know when to put out the bins, how the heating works or how to use the washing machine – so having the answers in writing (probably in digital form, sent along with the inventory) could well save your sanity.

Much as you don't want to be bothered every five minutes, you *do* want to be told about anything important (like a leak) – and you want your messages to be read. With HMO tenants, you're likely to get better results by adapting to their chosen method of communication: that could mean a WhatsApp group with all the tenants as members, or even Facebook.

Because of the higher potential for wear and tear (and the likelihood that everyone will leave it to each other to report an issue), regular inspections are more important than ever. If you provide a regular cleaner, make them an ally: encourage them to take photos of anything they spot that could be a concern, so that you find out what's going on without travelling back and forth to the property yourself every week.

However carefully you try to foresee everything that could provide a management challenge, there'll be a constant stream of issues you never could have anticipated. So note down every interaction you have with your tenants, and take time every few months to review your notes. Looking back, you'll be able to spot patterns and opportunities to prevent the same things from happening again – by updating the house manual, improving your processes or implementing new policies.

> *Pro tip: "Get a master key suite fitted, and install a key safe in the house which holds the master key. If a tenant calls saying they've locked themselves out of their room, just give them the safe code – then when you next visit, put the key back and change the safe code. Saves lots of time, and means that I only need to take one key for my visits too." –Jeremy Startup*

Lettings on hard mode

HMOs aren't necessarily something to shy away from, but they *are* lettings on hard mode: you're juggling more tenant relationships, and providing more facilities and services that you have responsibility for.

The key is to have the right expectations going in. If you approach it the same as you would a single let and try to bluff your way through, you'll find yourself resentfully dragged into a bewildering array of tasks – and the profit you make will seem extremely hard-earned.

But if you *expect* it to be hard work and commit from the start to making every aspect of managing the property as efficient as possible, you'll quickly get the measure of the task and it'll become easier in time.

BONUS 4:
LETTING A PROPERTY IN SCOTLAND

As I said back at the start, letting a property is governed by hundreds of regulations – pretty much guaranteeing that just when you get to grips with how something works, there'll be a change *somewhere* that has you scrambling to keep up.

It gets even more complicated what with housing being a devolved matter in Scotland, Wales and Northern Ireland. The changes are pretty minor in Wales and Northern Ireland, but significant in Scotland – and in late 2017, Scottish law will undergo a major shake-up.

This makes it a *particularly* terrible time to be writing a chapter about lettings in Scotland. So while I'll give an overview of the major differences here, bear in mind that *a lot of this is set to change later in the year*. The best way to stay up-to-date is to register your copy of this book at www.propertygeek.net/landlord, so that I can send you all future updates.

The big change to come

Last year, the The Private Housing (Tenancies) (Scotland) Act 2016 was passed, which is going to create a whole new type of tenancy – with some major and important differences. Old tenancies will continue as they are, but all new tenancies will be of this new type – called a Private Residential Tenancy (PRT).

The main change is that there will be no tenancy "term": a tenancy will continue until one party takes action to end it, with no need for it to be renewed.

The other big change is that the "no fault" eviction process (the equivalent of Section 21 in England and Wales) is being removed – so landlords won't be able to end a tenancy just because they feel like it. Instead, they'll have to use one of various "grounds" – such as at least three consecutive months of rent arrears, or wanting to take the property back to sell it.

It's thought that this will come into effect in Autumn 2017, but there's no set time at the moment.

In the meantime, the rest of this chapter covers the main ways in which letting in Scotland differs from England and Wales right now.

Landlord registration

All landlords in Scotland need to register with the local authority in which their property is located – even if you're going to be using a letting agent to do everything for you. After passing the "fit and proper person" test, your registration will be granted for three years – after which it will have to be renewed.

As well as registering yourself as a landlord with each local authority, you also need to register each property you decide to let.

You can register online at www.landlordregistrationscotland.gov.uk

Safety

Like in England and Wales, an EPC and an annual gas safety certificate are mandatory and must be given to the tenant before they move in. But unlike in England and Wales, an electrical safety inspection is also mandatory – and includes the need to test both the electrical installation (an Electrical Installation Condition Report) and the appliances that belong to you (a PAT test).

The electrical safety inspection must be renewed every five years, *or* (if sooner) at every change in tenancy. Copies of both the electrical and gas safety inspections must be given to tenants when they move in, and a new copy must be given every time they're updated during the tenancy.

The law in Scotland also sets a high standard for fire safety. According to the Repairing Standard (which is the basic level of repair that all rented properties must meet) there must be:

- A smoke alarm in the main room that's used for daytime living purposes

- A smoke alarm in every hallway and landing

- In total, at least one smoke alarm on every floor

- A heat detector in the kitchen

If the alarms were installed after September 2007 (even if they're replacing existing alarms), they should be interlinked and mains powered.

The requirements for carbon monoxide alarms are more stringent than in England and Wales too: there must be at least one carbon monoxide alarm in each property, including one in every room where there's a fuel-burning appliance (including boilers) and every bedroom that a flue passes through. And to comply, not just any alarm will do: it must have a sealed life-long battery.

More broadly, as well as meeting the Repairing Standard (which applies specifically to private landlords), all properties must also meet something called the Tolerable Standard – which applies to councils and housing associations too. Both standards are similar and impose a basic set of requirements, similar to a landlord's statutory repairing duties under the Housing Act in England

and Wales: maintaining the structure of the building, having adequate heating and hot water, maintaining installations for sanitation, and so on.

Tenancy types

Until the new system comes in, residential tenancies in Scotland are either "assured" or "short assured" – the rough equivalent of "assured" (AT) and "assured shorthold" (AST) in England.

Unlike in England, though, a tenancy doesn't default to "short assured": it defaults to "assured", which makes it much harder to get your property back. If you want the tenancy to be "short assured" (which you almost certainly do), you need to serve a particular notice on your tenant. The notice is called an AT5 form, which you can download by searching the gov.uk site for "AT5".

The AT5 notice must be served before the tenancy starts, and if there are joint tenants, each should be given a separate copy.

Tenancy administration and documentation

When advertising the property and searching for tenants in Scotland, bear in mind that you're not allowed to charge any kind of fees to tenants – just the rent, and the deposit.

At present, unlike in England and Wales, there's no need to establish a tenant's "Right To Rent" – but keep an eye out, as the intention seems to be to bring this in at some point.

Before the tenant moves in, you'll need to give them a Tenant Information Pack – which is roughly equivalent to the "How to rent" leaflet in England, but actually more useful.

You can download a copy from beta.gov.scot by searching "tenant information pack".

Protecting the deposit

The rules around protecting a tenant's deposit are broadly the same, but you'll need to place it with one of the three schemes that are particular to Scotland: MyDeposits Scotland (www.mydepositsscotland.co.uk), Safe Deposits Scotland (www.safedepositsscotland.com), and Letting Protection Service Scotland (www.lettingprotectionscotland.com).

Repairs during the tenancy

The property must meet the "repairing standard" throughout the tenancy – which is broadly similar to what's required in England and Wales. It's not too exacting: among other things, the property must meet a "tolerable standard" and be wind and watertight, which is a pretty low bar really.

If you can't clear this low bar, though, the tenant can refer the matter to the First Tier Tribunal, which can issue a "Repairing Standard Enforcement Order" (RSEO) commanding you to rectify whatever the problem is.

Ending the tenancy – at the end of the fixed term

The mechanism for ending a Short Assured tenancy is very similar to the system in England and Wales, but with some procedural tweaks and different terminology.

To use the "no fault" (equivalent of Section 21) procedure at or after the end of a fixed term, you need to serve two documents: a Notice to Quit, and a Section 33 notice.

Both notices can be served at the same time. The Notice to Quit comes into effect 40 days after service, but for a Section 33 it's two months – which means that in practice, it'll be two months before the tenant has to leave.

The Notice to Quit doesn't have to be in any particular form, but must contain:

- The length of notice given

- A statement saying that once the notice expires, the landlord must still get an order from the court before the tenant has to leave

- Information about where the tenant can get advice

The Section 33 notice must contain all the same information as above, and also state that possession is being sought under Section 33 of the Housing (Scotland) Act 1988.

You can download examples of both documents by searching the Shelter Scotland website at scotland.shelter.org.uk

Just like in England and Wales, if the tenant doesn't move out by the date stated on the notice, you will need to apply for a court order – which, again like England and Wales, will automatically be granted as long as you've done everything properly.

Ending the tenancy – before the end of the fixed term

Ending a tenancy early in Scotland involves – as elsewhere – giving one or more "grounds" for eviction, rather than using the "no fault" method.

The process involves issuing a Notice to Quit and a notice of proceedings form known as AT6 – which you can download by searching the gov.uk website. The Notice to Quit must be served before or at the same time as the AT6 – not after.

The AT6 form will state which "grounds" are being used – which are similar to England and Wales, and again consist of "mandatory" and "discretionary" grounds. And again, each ground requires a different amount of notice to be given.

Once the documents have been served and the notice period has expired, if the tenant hasn't left you then have six months to start court proceedings.

ACKNOWLEDGMENTS

In the course of writing this book, I've received advice, help and encouragement from *a lot* of people. It's safest to assume that the really good ideas are someone else's, and the mistakes are mine.

Special thanks to the team at Yellow Lettings for sharing their expertise and experiences, and to Matt Elder (www.uk-homefinder.net) for redefining the term "over-deliver" by replying to my request for a quick tip or two by sending me 10,000 words.

Tips and insights were also provided by over 50 Property Geek readers and members of The Property Hub community, including:

Mark Morris, Suki S Dhanda, Mat, Gareth Broom, Victoria Broom, Richard Springall, Kylie Ackers, Tom Smedley, Jeremy Startup, Vicky McMellon, Sanjay Kareer, Dolan Mullans, David Barker, Justyn Evans, Carol Duckfield, Brian Smart, Tory Ion-Webb, Nathan Browne, Ghan Varsani, Jo Lines, Ben Goddard, Joanne Dron, Kuldip Matoo, Muna Nwokolo, Ganesh Uttam, Floss Slade, Vientiene & Elizabeth Ta'eed, Richard Taylor, Adrian Bond, Malcolm Veall, Graham Page, Tony Ng, Matthew

Webster, Gary Brewin, Giles Dumont, Ha Ngo, Matthew Hall, Josh F, Jackie Moss, Tony, Lynn Stannard, Sanita Guddu, Chris McCormack, Ryan Cameron, Tomasz Slawek, Lokesh, Luke Voce, Jamie Harris, Dy Mahmood, Natalie from Essex, Jonathan Challis, Cheryl Poulter, Adam, Ugnius Arkusauskas, Rashta and Pravin Paratey.

And by this point nobody will still be reading, so I can safely admit that this book is only readable (and, indeed, finished) thanks to my wife, Mish Slade. She edited and laid out the book, wrote most of the best jokes, contributed a wealth of brilliant ideas, and supported me through my many near-meltdowns.

And she's pretty hot. So: sorry, she's taken – but you can still hire her to bring your business to life with her writing. Her website is at www.mortifiedcow.com